# Here with Us

## A Parish Guide to Welcoming People with Dementia

Michael Swan

**TWENTY-THIRD PUBLICATIONS**

**NOVALIS**

Published in Canada by Novalis
Publishing Office
1 Eglinton Avenue East, Suite 800
Toronto, Ontario, Canada
M4P 3A1
en.novalis.ca

Head Office
4475 Frontenac Street
Montréal, Québec, Canada
H2H 2S2

Cover design and layout: Audrey Wells
Cover image: iStockphoto

Cataloguing in Publication is available from Library and Archives Canada
ISBN: 978-2-89688-770-5

Published in the United States by
TWENTY-THIRD PUBLICATIONS
One Montauk Avenue, Suite 200
New London, CT 06320
(860) 437-3012 or (800) 321-0411
www.twentythirdpublications.com
ISBN: 978-1-62785-606-5

Cover design: Jeff McCall
Cover image: © Roxana Bashyrova / Shutterstock.com

Printed in Canada.

All rights reserved. No part of this publication may be reproduced, stored in a retrieval system, or transmitted in any form, or by any means, electronic, mechanical, photocopying, recording, or otherwise, without the written permission of the publisher.

We acknowledge the support of the Government of Canada.

5  4  3  2  1          24  23  22  21  20

FSC
www.fsc.org
MIX
Paper from responsible sources
FSC® C103567

In gratitude, this book is dedicated to
Our Lady of Lourdes Parish,
520 Sherbourne Street, Toronto.

Also by Michael Swan

*Written on My Heart:*
*Classic Prayers in the Modern World*
(Novalis, 2019)

*Out of the Cold: A History of Caring*
(Catholic Register Books, 2015)

# Contents

Confronting Reality: *What's the problem here?* ...................... 7

Jesus Knows Our Reality: *Reading the Gospel for dementia* ................................................................. 11

The Reality Code: *What science tells us about dementia* ................................................................. 19

The Caring Reality: *Why we care* ................................ 33

Real Planning: *How to begin acknowledging parishioners with dementia* ................................................................. 39

Reality Out There: *Where to find those who need you most* ................................................................. 45

The Architecture of Reality: *Getting your building dementia-ready* ................................................................. 51

Real Liturgy: *The source and summit of caring* ....................... 59

Physical Reality: *Health is our collective concern* ................... 67

The Reality of Care: *Beyond the patient, who we're helping* ................................................................. 73

Real Dying: *The new legal and cultural landscape* ................... 79

Really Caring: *Courage in our encounter with dementia* ....... 89

Sources ................................................................. 94

# Confronting Reality

## What's the problem here?

The statistics speak for themselves.

Every year another 76,000 Canadians are diagnosed with some form of dementia. In 2020 there were over half a million Canadians with dementia. By 2030 there will be close to 1 million. More than 7 percent of Canadians will at some point live with dementia.[1] In the year 2036, 3 percent of all Canadians alive will have a form of dementia, to some degree.[2]

In the U.S. nearly 6 million people are living with dementia now, and it counts as the sixth leading cause of death. By 2030 there will be 8.4 million Americans over the age of 65 living with the most common form of dementia, Alzheimer's. By 2050 it will be 13.8 million.[3,4]

American doctors are overwhelmed. In 2020, primary care physicians reported that 40 percent of their current patients were 65 or older. On average, 13 percent of those older patients had been diagnosed with dementia. There are still doctors – 22 percent – who say they had no residency training in treating patients with dementia. But even worse is the fact that more than half describe their dementia training as "very little."

So they refer to specialists, when they are available. More than half (55 percent) of American doctors told an Alzheimer's Association survey that there aren't enough doctors in their area to meet the demand.[5]

The World Economic Forum projects that by 2050, there will be 152 million of us worldwide living with dementia. By 2030, the health care cost of caring for this one category of illness will top $2 trillion. If dementia care were a country, it would be the world's 18th-largest economy.[6]

We live longer, but we don't necessarily live better. One quarter of Canadians will be older than 65 by 2036. Over 50,000 Canadians with dementia right now are living in hospitals.[7] This is not ideal. In 2020, two thirds of nursing home residents had a diagnosis of dementia, and nursing home staff are ill-equipped to care for them.[8]

Does the church care? Jesuit Fr. John Siberski, a medical doctor in Boston who specializes in geriatrics, thought one good measure of how much the church cares might be to see how many seminaries and theology faculties in English-speaking North America have programs or courses to prepare priests, deacons and lay ministers to engage the elderly – precisely the people who take up the most space in Sunday morning pews. He couldn't find one.

"They've all got courses in youth ministry. You can major in youth ministry. Not one place had even a course on the elderly," Siberski told me.

Deacon Matt Dineen, who describes himself as a "dementia champion," occasionally takes his wife, Lisa, to Mass in Ottawa. She lives apart from her family in a long-term care facility with a severe early onset form of dementia. Lisa sometimes stands when everyone else is kneeling. She sometimes vocalizes (she no longer speaks) in response to what's happening around her. Dineen has just about had it with the looks his family gets from others up and down the pew.

"I just wish the people around would say 'OK, she has dementia,' and that they would be fine with that," Dineen said. "I would like to see dementia-friendly Masses. I know that's probably a way off."

"Most churches will have people with dementia in their congregations. They would like to help, but they don't always know how," said Fay Sampson, the British author of the 2017 book *Prayers for Dementia*.[9]

Sampson has seen parishes ignore people with dementia simply because they don't know what to say or how to behave with people whose memory problems have begun to interfere with ordinary thinking and conversation.

"It's important to seek out those with dementia and talk to them, because they find it harder to initiate conversations than they once did," Sampson said.

Nobody is asking parishes to solve society's looming dementia crisis. Parishes are not health care institutions. They are not governments, which could fund community health services. But parishes cannot sit this out, hoping somebody else solves it. They must play their part.

"It comes down to that whole essence of the mission of the church," Catholic author and retired health care leader Michelle O'Rourke told me. "You know, we're preaching and teaching and healing. We forget that healing part."

If Jesus spent most of his ministry on earth healing the sick, can parishes really turn around and say healing is somebody else's business?

The great Sr. Nuala Kenny – Order of Canada, physician, professor of medicine and founder of the Dalhousie University department of bioethics – tells anybody who will listen about the difference between healing and curing. Curing is just about the mechanics and biochemistry of our bodies – adjusting elements of our physical being for more efficient and effective performance. Healing brings our very selves into alignment with creation around us and its creator. For a Christian, healing does not so much bind our wounds as bind us closer to God, making us whole. That's what Jesus did and still does with lepers, the blind and the outcast.

At the Alzheimer Society of Canada, they want to help. They run a program to train volunteers and community leaders in dementia issues – how to make their buildings and their programs ready to welcome those with dementia. It's called the Dementia Friendly Communities Initiative.[10] They've had some interest from individual United Church, Presbyterian and Anglican congregations. They've never had a single phone call or email from a Catholic parish or diocese, according to Alzheimer Society of Canada spokesperson Roseanne Meandro.

In the U.S., the Alzheimer's Association[11] has created a network of hundreds of faith ambassadors who connect their churches with local community resources. The association also sponsors "Shedding Light" breakfasts, where clergy and community leaders learn about the disease and ways they can support families.[12]

If you feel you need help, you're right. The task is immense. The good news is that help is out there. It is hoped that this book will help your parish figure out what help it needs and where it might find it.

# Jesus Knows Our Reality

## Reading the Gospel for Dementia

"Just as you did it to one of the least of these who are members of my family, you did it to me," the king says to his subjects in Jesus' parable known as "The Judgment of the Nations" (Matt. 25:31-46).

Who is less in our society than those who struggle to remember, struggle to speak, struggle to understand? We live in a competitive, me-first kind of society that honours and rewards the smart, the quick, the ones with the right answers. As this disease takes hold, the familiar becomes unfamiliar. People among us with dementia become strangers – strangers to themselves, strangers to those who love them, strangers to the world.

If we take Jesus' parable seriously, it is the strangers who are at the centre of the story. Whatever happens to the strangers is the measure of who we are. What happens to strangers among us happens to all of us. We are judged by our treatment of strangers, and we don't want to "go away into eternal punishment" (Matt. 25:46).

The section of the Gospel of Matthew that culminates in this parable is set up to answer a question. "What will the kingdom of heaven be like?" However, the answer isn't in the parables. Jesus answers this question with his life, his passion and his resurrection. These stories are instead preparation for the drama to come.

The kingdom of heaven is like a life that has endured suffering, injustice and death but rises again to be with us always.

In this series of three parables that take up all of chapter 25 of Matthew's gospel, each story ends in a harsh judgment, then final and unforgiving banishment. Five wise bridesmaids refuse to share their oil and send the foolish bridesmaids away on an impossible search for lamp oil in the middle of the night (Matt. 25:1-13). The careful and cautious steward of a single talent of the king's gold is upbraided and thrown into outer darkness for doing precisely what an honest steward is supposed to do – holding onto the king's money and keeping it safe (Matt. 25:14-30).

Ultimately, we get this king, who divides the population between the deserving and the undeserving, the good and the bad. "I was a stranger and you did not welcome me, naked and you did not give me clothing, sick and in prison and you did not visit me," he tells those on his left. The king accuses these people, then condemns them to "eternal punishment" (Matt. 25:31-46).

Let go of the idea that this king is God. Most of us have heard too many sermons that mistake parables for allegory. This king is an absolute authority unto himself, as kings are. When we let go of this notion of the king as God, dividing and condemning, it frees us to imagine ourselves hearing the story for the first time. It frees us also from a distorted, inadequate image of God. We are free to ask, how do we see ourselves in the story?

Do we really believe that the kingdom Jesus came to inaugurate will be a place of harsh judgment and immediate exclusion? No, that's our life now – or at least it is the lives of too many of us. The point of Jesus' last parables in Matthew's gospel is to force us to recognize this cruelty. As he spins each tale, Jesus forces us to choose sides. Do we identify with the foolish bridesmaids, sympathize with the beleaguered and cornered steward, recoil at the accusation that we have betrayed the king's family and fear the judgment that is to follow?

I can't help but think, "I don't want to be the one sent out into the darkness with no lamp oil, or humiliated by the king just for doing my job, or punished for being unable to solve problems the king should have solved." After all, if these naked, starving, thirsty people in prison are members of the king's household, then why didn't he protect his own family? Why do I have to do it for him? I don't have the king's unlimited power and resources.

Jesus tells these stories because he wants to remind us of how we have been cast away, humiliated and abandoned – how we have been judged. He wants us to feel that sting of judgment and the outrage of being accused by arrogant and careless people in power. He wants to remind us how quickly and easily the powerful dispose of people and problems. He wants us to remember who we are – we who have been humiliated, judged, pushed away and ignored.

Imagine being part of Jesus' audience – whether in the courtyard of the temple or a village synagogue or a dusty marketplace under Roman guard. We look around and see ourselves as one of the judged, surrounded by others who share our fear and shame.

As Jesus tells that last story, I think he knows his audience all want to identify with the good, honourable people on the king's right (the sheep). But at the same time, we fear we might be more like the selfish, dishonourable people (the goats) on the left. But what if we are neither? What if we are those tired, thirsty strangers who arrive in town without a cloak to keep warm? What if we're the people who fall ill or are thrown in prison? These forgotten members of the king's family are voiceless in the story. Have you felt voiceless? Silenced?

Now imagine you are living with dementia. Have you been humiliated, judged, pushed away and ignored? Are you a person who gets treated as a problem, the way the foolish bridesmaids and the cautious steward have been? Are you dependent on the whims of either the honourable people on the king's right or the dishonourable ones standing to the left?

I believe the people with dementia in our communities are in fact more like the king's starving, naked family, left hungry, thirsty and alone by some, but clothed and fed and kept company by others. Like the king's family, they have no choice to make. They are voiceless – either chosen for welcome and hospitality or not chosen at all. It's a precarious place to be, waiting for the king's final judgment.

There is hope hidden beneath this painful experience. These parables prepare us for Christ's passion. After he tells the crowd stories of arrogant kings and mean teenage girls casting ordinary people out into darkness, he tells his disciples what will happen at the Passover – how he will be accused, humiliated and unjustly punished (Matt. 26:1-2).

Is that hope? It is for us who know Jesus alive with us and in us. The passion cannot be separated from the resurrection. If you bought this book, you are searching for resurrection in your experience of suffering through your own cognitive decline or as you care for someone with dementia. You believe the resurrection is here, now and in the future, for yourself and for your parish as it embraces the suffering of those with dementia.

The people in your parish with dementia aren't a problem best left in outer darkness or cast aside. They are still human – more human and more Christ-like – through their suffering. They are often imprisoned in a shrinking world, defined by the few places they can safely navigate and the fewer and fewer people who will ever stop to say hello.[13] Whether they have lived perfect or imperfect lives, whether they were geniuses or not, they have done nothing to deserve the chains now draped across their minds.

When these parishioners look around during a long homily, what do they see? Do they see a community that is there for them? Or do they fear a crowd of careless, angry tyrants sending them into outer darkness? Is the crowd around them holding itself back, hoping they will never face judgment?

We are not such tyrants, we hope. Nor cowards hoping judgment falls on others. Our parishes are full of genuinely good people. As a parish, we need to examine ourselves and our relationships – not for the sake of our own purity or salvation, but for the sake of the kingdom Jesus proclaimed to us.

Jesus asks, over and over, who is our neighbour? Who is the stranger among us? Who is blessed and who is cursed? In the Sermon on the Plain, Jesus shocks us with how he defines the cursed.

"But woe to you who are rich,
 for you have received your consolation.
"Woe to you who are full now,
 for you will be hungry.
"Woe to you who are laughing now,
 for you will mourn and weep.
"Woe to you when all speak well of you,
 for that is what their ancestors did to the false prophets."
(Luke 6:24-26)

Have good Catholics just been cursed by Jesus? I hope not. We are here to bless the frail, elderly, confused woman sitting alone, one pew over. So how do we do that?

At the altar, the priest lays out bread and wine, prays in words handed down from Jesus before he faced his torturers. The priest lifts the chalice, lifts the bread. It is the real presence. It is Christ here and now among us. This is what the kingdom of God is like, and it's real.

Reality, whenever it touches us, demands of each and every person responsibility. When we really become a mother or father, really become a husband or wife, we must take responsibility for our lives and for each other. All our sacraments are part of the larger reality of Christ's real presence in the eucharist. The real presence on the altar is the gateway to any Christian understanding of reality and Christian responsibility. There it is, the kingdom of God.

So our responsibility to that stranger down the pew who keeps opening and closing her purse, looking up and down the aisle, frozen halfway between kneeling and standing, is to be the real presence for her and with her. Dementia demands the real presence of each and every one of us, the real presence of all of us together, to reconstitute the presence of God in her life.

Can we do this? Can we take a pass and hope somebody else, better qualified and better trained, will take it on? If we try, who will tell us whether we have succeeded? How much real presence will be enough for her? What if we are not real enough, or present enough, to reconnect her with the world she once knew and understood?

This book, this author, can't definitively answer these questions. They are what church professionals call eschatological questions. They concern the end times, the sum of all things, the ultimate. All of us live in the midst of final judgment, but we are not the judge. We have no business guessing at the judge's last dispensation.

But we should be assured that ultimate solutions for dementia, just like the ultimate healing of the world, are up to God. He is the end-times judge and we trust this judge. Our judge has been judged, condemned, crucified. He is one of us – we who wince at the harsh judgments in those last parables of Matthew's gospel. He is present with and in each person with dementia. Are we willing to be present, really present, with Jesus? Will we play our part?

It's a hard part to play, not knowing how much good we're doing or how to fix the problem. We would prefer certainty. In the 21st century, we have mostly chosen to reason, to analyze and to know the answers. We want to be right. We measure ourselves by how often we have the right answer. We shun the contagion of wrong answers, half answers, confusion and forgetfulness. This preference for clarity and precision, hard facts and science, is not wrong. But it's not enough.

What is enough? The kingdom Jesus announced in his life and in his resurrection is enough. The real presence of Jesus, here and now in your parish, is enough for parishioners with dementia.

As you read what follows, begin to think of a parish dementia committee. Begin to imagine how your community might practically, concretely choose life and length of days for each other. Imagine your parish really present in the lives of its weakest and poorest members.

# The Reality Code

## What science tells us about dementia

No one would suggest that to be a family caregiver, a friend, a parish volunteer or a pastor of someone with dementia requires an advanced degree in neuroscience. You don't have to be a doctor, a nurse, a dietician or a physiotherapist to care for someone. Pretending to take on these roles will only get in the way of doing what you, their friend, should do.

But neither is it helpful to sit in fearful ignorance. Not knowing what the person with dementia is experiencing or why it is happening is certainly a barrier.

Too often, we substitute vague cultural assumptions about dementia for what science has learned over this last century of intensive study. Family memories of caring for a long-gone great aunt, or the advice of a neighbour who knew somebody once who was caring for their mother, is unlikely to clarify our understanding or inform our care.

"With the whole question of Alzheimer's, people need to know that none of this is imagined; none of it is something they did to bring it on," said Jesuit gerontologist Fr. John Siberski.

People ask Siberski, "What can I do to prevent it?" He has to tell them there are no magic pills or vitamins. Good health, particularly good cardiovascular health, can minimize the risk. But there are 55 different kinds of dementia. Science is still discovering new things about it. Everything from genetics to diet has something to say about how these diseases progress. So what are the chances there's going to be a fix – some simple, one-time technical solution that just makes it go away?

Science constantly makes our lives better, but not because it makes problems disappear. The most important thing science does is change our relationship to our problems. There will be breakthroughs for dementia patients, but even after those breakthroughs there will still be dementia patients.

"It is critical to understand what's going on with the brain, with the body," said Siberski. "Because it's going to have a tremendous effect on one's understanding, one's relationship with God in prayer."

The disease will change us, certainly. And as we change, all of our relationships change, including our relationship with God. Understanding the science can take some of the pressure off that relationship. We need not blame God for mysterious and random misfortune if science shows us that our tragedy can at least be named and understood.

Science provides us with categories and vocabulary. Put to use, scientific language and habits of thought lead to insight. Insight can be the foundation for care.

Words often fail the dementia patient. But not just *their* words. Sometimes it's *our* words – the words we apply to them, or that even just float in the air around them. Our words are often a betrayal. Here again, substituting science for unconscious cultural assumptions helps us put care in the place of fear, dismay, frustration and defeat.

People with dementia might not remember your name. They might not remember what you said. But they usually remember how you made them feel. This emotional memory is expressed even in the advanced stages of dementia. A negative memory will show up as fear when certain people enter the room, or joy when others show up.

So perhaps we stop talking to someone who can't form a sentence or find the words to answer. We're not being cruel. It's just easier that way. But once she becomes furniture amid other people's conversations, who is she? Her present condition does not erase the life she has lived. Her disease doesn't make her any less herself.

The language we use about and around the person with dementia should reflect this simple scientific insight: dementia is a medical condition, the result of pathologies and not human weakness.

In this book I don't use the word *demented*, even though it is the grammatically correct nounal adjective to describe those living with dementia. We all grew up with Dr. Demento[14] and 1,000 other associations with the word that can only be described as stigmatizing. If the people who have dementia are going to be cared for in our homes, our institutions and our parishes they cannot be stigmatized.

Roman soldiers who inflicted the stigmata on Christ's hands, feet and side were not celebrating his humanity, even if today these wounds are our pathway into God's saving incarnation.

It is not always so obvious when and how people are stigmatized. We're not necessarily talking about crude, cruel abuse. But there's an atmosphere that surrounds the stigmatized. Rather than recognizing people, we file them away into a category. We throw them, people, into a kind of mental bin of words and images, full of all the things we fear and despise. Of course, it helps us to know what we fear, but only so that we can avoid it. It helps to point out what we despise, but only to separate it from ourselves. It doesn't help us to care for anything or anyone.

Science can cut through this atmosphere. It can bring clarity and courage.

"Be not afraid," St. Pope John Paul II said in his first address as pope in 1978. He repeated those words often. For the great Polish pope, a courageous faith was essential to becoming truly human. Fear is the opposite of reason.[15] Overcoming fear is also necessary for any person or community that aspires to care for anyone else.

Pope Francis has often warned us that we live in a throwaway culture. He's not just talking about our preference for disposable consumer goods. He is even more concerned by our willingness to dispose of people we no longer find useful.[16] In the pope's vision, we wound ourselves with our quick and casual impulse to stigmatize those we name and shun. We wound ourselves collectively. It is a poorer, more limited civilization that can only admire useful people. Only a tawdry parody of civilization depends on getting rid of people who make us uncomfortable.[17] Communities that can only accept the pretty, the perfect and the useful are soon not a community at all.

Valuing people for who they are, before they show us what they can do, is not easy. Caregivers, left alone without support, will almost inevitably give in to frustration. The language of science can help. We betray people with our lazy use of words and the vague, half-understood meanings we attribute to them. If we don't know how to describe or think precisely about dementia, how can we know how to be there, present, with those who live with the disease?

Science helps us to understand that people are not their diseases. That one little insight will not relieve every stress of caring for a person with dementia, but it reframes the relationship. It's a start. So let's start with some definitions.

This book uses the word **dementia** to describe the broad sweep of life-limiting illnesses that affect cognition and memory. The word **Alzheimer's** is reserved for speaking of this specific disease.

None of these diseases or conditions described below – which are either a form of dementia or a contributor to complex dementias – are part of the normal aging process. The risks of falling ill may increase with age, but the diseases we explore here have specific causes. They are not just a bad way of growing old.

This is good news. The more we know about the cause of a disease, the greater the chances science will discover a cure or (more likely) that the daily and constant practice of medicine will teach us therapies that will restore a little bit of the life these patients have been losing.

As I write, the various sciences of dementia – neuroscience, genetics, biochemistry, gerontology, psychology and more – are hammering away our ignorance. By the time this text gets through editing and printing, there may be new drugs, new therapies and new diagnostic tools. But here is where we stand for now.

**Alzheimer's disease** is the most common form of dementia. In casual speech, many will substitute Alzheimer's for dementia in general. But this is wrong, because it perpetuates the assumption that all dementias are the same.

Anywhere from 60 to 80 percent of people with dementia have Alzheimer's. But a substantial number of these also have, at the same time, other forms or causes of dementia.

Specific to Alzheimer's are tiny, dense deposits of proteins scattered through the brain. As these deposits rise to excessive levels they become toxic – deadly to brain cells. The deposits are called "amyloid plaque." Amyloid is a kind of protein that occurs naturally in every normal brain, though we don't know precisely why it's there or what it does. Plaque is anything built up in layers, from cholesterol to yellowing layers of bacteria on our teeth.

Amyloid protein builds up into plaque when brain cells can no longer discard the protein. Researchers are still trying to discover why brain cells in Alzheimer's patients are unable to expel these amyloid proteins, as they normally would. Is it because the proteins have folded? Or have the proteins folded because they have not been expelled?[18]

Alzheimer's disease also generates fibrous clumps or tangles of a protein called tau. Tau proteins are important and useful in healthy brains. They carry nutrients and other essential compounds to various areas of the brain. They are supply lines leading to the front lines of thinking, including that most important part of thinking, memory. As Alzheimer's advances, tau proteins fold, clump and collapse into neurofibrillary tangles.

These two physical features of Alzheimer's disease interact with each other. When plaque surrounds a neuron, it dies. Tangles are found inside neurons where they get in the way of the cell's ability to flush out and recycle proteins, again causing the cell to die.[19]

As cell death progresses, patients suffer a loss of brain tissue and brain mass.[20] The disease begins to appear in the medial temporal lobe of the brain, most often the hippocampus. Science has known for a long time that the hippocampus plays a central role in learning and memory. This disease starts there and moves outward.

But that doesn't mean a computerized axial tomography (CAT) scan or positron emission tomography (PET) scan, even if it can show a loss of brain tissue, can tell you whether someone has Alzheimer's. As of now, the only way to definitively diagnose Alzheimer's is to cut out pieces of the brain, put the tissue under a microscope and look for the plaque and tangles that characterize the disease. Obviously, this is best done after the patient has died.[21]

But we are eating away at the edges of this limitation. A particular application of PET scans called amyloid imaging has been found useful in clinical trials. For those who can pay, it's available in some U.S. cities. In Canada, it's considered experimental and not covered by provincial health insurance.

An alternative to PET amyloid imaging may be emerging in retinal scans. Our retinas are made up of the same sorts of cells that attract amyloid plaque build-ups in the brain. American researchers working on the Atlas of Retinal Imaging in Alzheimer's Study, or ARIAS, think they may be able to find structural changes in the retina that could give clues to which brains are developing or are likely to develop Alzheimer's.[22]

A cheap and reliable blood test for Alzheimer's, one that could detect the disease years before symptoms are apparent,[23] is very likely in the next few years. That test will change the landscape for research. But it hasn't happened yet.

In the meantime, all doctors can do is run a number of tests that might rule out other causes of dementia. Once that has been done, we might be able to safely say that Mum probably has Alzheimer's. But if it hasn't been done, it can be a grave error to treat someone experiencing dementia as if they have this particular incurable, deadly disease when in fact they may have another, more treatable condition.

Alzheimer's is deadly – a terminal disease that always kills the patient. It isn't just forgetfulness. It leads to physical, system-wide failures throughout the body. Alzheimer's patients often die of infection, because their bodies have lost the ability to fight off infections that a non-Alzheimer's patient could easily recover from, or because they pick up infections that other people would not get. Patients die of aspiration pneumonia. That is what happens when food or liquid goes down the windpipe instead of the esophagus. This damages the lungs and invites infection that develops into pneumonia.[24]

In most people, it's a slow-moving disease. In the early stages, it doesn't seem like anything is terribly wrong. Everybody forgets names, misplaces their keys, gets distracted and confused. Not everybody who is looking for the pair of glasses that was sitting on their face half a minute ago has Alzheimer's. But later this person may begin to search their brain for the names of common, everyday objects – things they've known how to name since they learned to talk, like sandwich or milk. They still know what a sandwich is and that milk is something they're supposed to drink. But they can't come up with the word.

There are other ways language can become a problem. People who speak two languages may lose the ability to construct a sentence in their second language.

Eventually, there may also be emotional changes – often a kind of tamping down of emotions and a lack of emotional engagement. This might be depression – a natural response to losing capabilities once taken for granted – or it might be the disease itself.[25]

At some point this person will have trouble living on their own. Choosing the right clothes to wear on a winter's morning, remembering to eat, to take medications, how to get to the corner store and buy milk – all these become impossible tasks. The names of grandchildren, daughters and sons disappear.

Even over the course of a day, a person's ability to cope can swing wildly. A morning that begins with making tea, quiet conversation, enjoying a song on the radio can end with tears of rage, frustration and finally exhaustion – sundowning.[26] By the later stages of the disease, people find themselves permanently disoriented, which can lead to wandering.[27] Even the most attentive, patient and dedicated family caregiver can no longer manage this situation alone. Institutional long-term care is often the best option for both patient and family.

**Vascular dementia** is probably the easiest form of dementia to understand, even if it is almost impossible to treat. The vascular system delivers blood to all parts of our bodies. If it fails, or slows down moving blood into the brain, then brain cells aren't just missing the blood flow. They're not getting oxygen – the most important cargo carried in blood. Without oxygen, cells die, including brain cells.

One does not need a medical degree to guess there's a risk of stroke in any vascular system breakdown near or in the brain. But there are less dramatic symptoms that build up over a longer period. As the oxygen flow slows and brain cells die, people gradually find it more and more difficult to make plans, to choose, to make decisions or to get organized. It might at first seem like normal aging when a person's gait changes to a more plodding, less elegant style of walking, or when they have problems finding their balance standing up. But these are developments that should be reported to a doctor.[28]

Vascular dementia does not exist in exclusion of Alzheimer's or other forms of dementia. Vascular system failures can combine with other dementias to make them worse.

If it were easy to fix the vascular system in the brain, such a treatment would probably benefit every single one of us over the age of 40. But there's no pill that can reverse the damage and restore function. Doctors may prescribe a class of medications called cholinesterase inhibitors. Some of the commercial versions come with alluring and hopeful sounding names such as "Cognex" and "Exelon." They are not cures.

This class of drugs limits the presence of cholinesterase in the brain. This chemical is normally there to break down another chemical called acetylcholine. Acetylcholine speeds messages between neurons to activate muscles and initiate other functions of the body. This chemical is part of the system that makes us sit up and pay attention. It gets us ready to react to all kinds of stimuli. By limiting cholinesterase (the chemical that breaks down acetylcholine), the drug leaves more acetylcholine in the brain. This has the potential to make the patient more attentive.

But being more attentive only allows the patient to cope with dementia a little better. It doesn't cure dementia. And there are important side effects to these drugs, including low blood pressure, constriction of the pupils in the eyes, increased sweat, saliva and tears, a slow heart rate, mucus secretion in the respiratory tract and constriction of the airways.[29]

There are two forms of vascular system breakdown involved in dementia.

1. Small-vessel disease leads to **subcortical dementia**. Small vessels in the brain become stiff and twisted, and this strangles the flow of blood to the brain.
2. That fateful protein amyloid builds up in the brain's blood vessels to cause **cerebral amyloid angiopathy**. Amyloid plaques get in the way of brain function. This is characteristic of Alzheimer's disease.

**Parkinson's disease** is something we've all seen – the old guy with the shakes. But it is in fact much more complex and it manifests itself in ways that can be categorized as dementia. Anywhere from half to three quarters of Parkinson's cases develop into dementia. The dementia phase of the disease usually appears about 10 years after onset of Parkinson's.

It all starts in the substantia nigra, the "black substance" deep in the brain stem. It appears black, at least in comparison to the rest of the brain, because of neuromelanin and a concentrated knot of dopaminergic neurons. Neuromelanin is similar to the melatonin that gives our skin colour. In our brains it plays a protective role, binding itself to toxic metals that threaten the integrity of the brain. Dopaminergic neurons generate dopamine, and dopamine is good.

Dopamine is part of the reward and motor-control systems in the brain. In part, it can activate production of serotonin and acetylcholine. If the dopamine-producing cells in the substantia nigra break down and not enough dopamine is being produced or circulated in the brain, serotonin levels drop. This manifests itself in a feeling of sadness and, over a longer period, depression. Low dopamine also results in lower acetylcholine production, which manifests as inattention, big swings in alertness, and visual hallucinations. Mix them all together and you've got dementia – Parkinsonian dementia.

Levodopa can help with the tremors. Cholinesterase inhibitors can even out attention. Selective serotonin reuptake inhibitors (our friends Paxil, Cipralex and others) can help with mood. The drugs don't cure Parkinson's, but they can make it much more bearable and a little less like dementia.

**Pick's disease** isn't a term doctors commonly use anymore. It is one of the group of frontotemporal dementias caused by damage to the forward third of the brain, the frontal lobe. In terms of behaviour, it starts with a turn toward the argumentative and confrontational, especially with family or those closest to the patient. These changes in personality make it different from Alzheimer's. But like Alzheimer's, it progresses through a period of aphasia – the inability to recall or find the right word. It's highly hereditary and often begins earlier than other forms of dementia, in people between the ages of 45 and 65.

**Frontotemporal dementia** is a category, rather than a single disease. There are six different types of dementia that fall into the category of frontotemporal dementia, but together these account for about 20 percent of dementia cases, second only to Alzheimer's. From Pick's disease to forms of degenerative motor neuron disease associated with amyotrophic lateral sclerosis (ALS), they have in common degeneration in the frontal lobe. They all affect behaviour and language. These are often relatively early onset, claiming younger victims, and they develop gradually. There is no cure, but some behaviours can be managed with selective serotonin reuptake inhibitors such as Celexa, Paxil and Zoloft – drugs we associate with treatment for depression.

**Lewy body dementia** sits at the crossroads between Alzheimer's and Parkinson's. It's caused by a buildup of protein called alpha-synuclein inside the brain's nerve cells. These deposits are called "Lewy bodies." Whether by itself or in combination with Alzheimer's, or in combination with Parkinson's, Lewy body dementia accounts for between 5 and 15 percent of dementias.

As the Lewy bodies build up in the brain, people lose memory function, language comprehension, an ability to think logically or make calculations. This can happen quickly and is often accompanied by hallucinations, which can range from seeing people who aren't there to seeing faces, animals or words in carpet or wallpaper patterns. Hallucinations, and the confusion that accompanies them, can be very distressing. Doctors may prescribe medications to control these symptoms, but there is no cure.

**Mild cognitive impairment** is not a disease but a description of the state of a person's brain function. It is what it says it is – thinking less well than normal. To qualify as mild cognitive impairment, the condition must be more significant than normal aging. It may be an indication that Alzheimer's or another dementia is on its way, but it ain't necessarily so. Sometimes mild cognitive impairment remains mild. Sometimes it gets better with a better diet, more exercise, lower blood pressure, more and richer social interactions.[30]

**Vitamin deficiency** is obviously not a disease. People who don't have or retain enough vitamin A, C, B-12, D and folate may have a medical condition, or they may have a poor diet. Extremely low levels of vitamin D have been associated with Alzheimer's and other dementias.[31] But there's no evidence that taking vitamins can either reverse or prevent dementia.[32] One common vitamin-related dementia is **Wernicke-Korsakoff syndrome**. Usually, though not always, this is a consequence of severe, prolonged alcohol abuse. The brain fails to absorb vitamin B1, which the brain needs as an energy source. Without B1, thought processes don't quite make it to completion.[33]

**Thyroid dementia** is one of a small number of dementias that can be reversed to some extent. Hypothyroidism can have effects that, left untreated, mimic dementia. Two to 5 percent of people over 65 have shrunken, deteriorating thyroid glands that are not producing enough of the hormones their thyroid is supposed to supply to the body. Left untreated, thyroid hormone deficiency can result in hypertension (high blood pressure), hyperlipidemia (elevated levels of fats, cholesterol and triglycerides in the blood), myxedema coma (a slowing down of both body and brain function), and cognitive deficits. A prescription for Levo-T, Synthroid or some other form of levothyroxine can have a dramatic effect.

**Medication interactions** are not a form of dementia, but they can look a lot like it. Whenever a person seems to be more confused and is having trouble coping or understanding, a doctor should review their medications.

# The Caring Reality

## Why we care

Canada's most unrecognized and ignored theologian never taught theology and never wrote any books of theology. But she had one original, penetrating and thoroughly convincing insight.

Sr. Simone Roach of the Sisters of St. Martha discovered in prayer and in a lifetime of nursing and teaching that what makes us human is care. We cannot be human unless we care. It's not opposable thumbs or a big, complex brain that make us human. Rather, it is caring for someone or something. It is a lifetime of accumulated care for others. Though she never said it like this, we participate in the life of the Trinity by taking up God's care for creation. We play a part in this whenever we are cared for or care for others.[34]

Roach taught nursing. Indeed, she practically built the nursing faculty at St. Francis Xavier University in Antigonish, Nova Scotia. She was part of a generation of nursing educators who raised nursing up from a craft or trade to a profession. In 1980 she was asked to oversee the writing of the first code of ethics for Canadian nurses.[35] Lawyers and doctors have long had codes of ethics because that is the sort of public declaration of responsibility, to others and to society, that makes a profession a profession.

The code of ethics Roach's committee developed in the 1980s has been revised and recast a dozen times or more in the last 35 years. The code remains, as it should be, very specific to nursing. But the insight at the base of that code – that we are caring beings – has wide application beyond nursing.

No parish, Catholic school, lay movement, diocese or volunteer should seek to replace or reproduce the professional medical care nurses provide. But they should care, and they should think about how they care for the people in their communities who live with dementia.

Roach came up with "six Cs" of caring. Any Catholic parish, or your parish dementia committee, could ask itself how it fulfills each of these six categories of caring – compassion, competence, conscience, confidence, commitment and creativity.

**Compassion** is the easy one. We know the meaning of the word – "to suffer with." We know that the "passion" part of the word is exactly how we describe Christ's suffering, from his trials before the Sanhedrin, Pilate and Herod through his scourging and crucifixion. The "com" prefix means "with." Compassion for the person with dementia is simply a matter of knowing with certainty that her suffering is our suffering. *She* doesn't struggle to communicate; *we* struggle. *She* doesn't fear the obstacles in her path as she walks; *we* fear them. *She* doesn't burn with shame if she is treated and talked to like a naughty child; *we* burn with shame.

Easy to understand, but not easy to do. If the daily practice of compassion isn't easy, perhaps we should pray for those we have failed. Perhaps we should confess our hardness of heart. Maybe, when we receive the eucharist, we should remember that this communion with Christ is also communion with everyone who suffers – including the stranger in the pew who struggles to say, "Peace be with you."

**Competence** is more difficult, because it raises questions about what competence we have and which competences we could acquire. Parish volunteers, sisters, priests and bishops are not (ordinarily) gerontologists, neurologists, psychologists or occupational therapists, and they should not try to fill these roles. But to serve a community, we must recognize that genuine communities are built on bonds of friendship. If a parish is not competent in friendship, it is not a parish. Perhaps it is legally a parish, but functionally it's a club with a rather ornate clubhouse.

"You are my friends if you do what I command you," Jesus tells his disciples. "I do not call you servants any longer, because the servant does not know what the master is doing; but I have called you friends, because I have made known to you everything that I have heard from my Father. You did not choose me but I chose you" (John 15:14-16).

If we are chosen to be friends, we are challenged to be competent in friendship. So the question this category of caring raises for the parish dementia committee is "How do we act on our friendship with those living with dementia?"

**Conscience** is too often defined in defence of personal, private, individual acts. Simplistic catechism descriptions of conscience are all about figuring out what to say when you are alone on your knees in a confessional.[36] But neither the good nor the evil abroad in our world ever depends on any one of us individually. It depends on those larger movements and structures in our world – larger movements and structures we are caught up in. Nobody confesses that they burned down the Amazon, blanched the great coral reefs or extinguished thousands of species from the planet. But we were there. We were part of it. Such destruction is evil and it happened on our watch. Nobody confesses to propping up an economy built on greed, but we buy things we don't need and define ourselves by the things we own and the debts we accumulate. We didn't will this evil. But we have been part of the culture that made these choices.

Original sin is not an event that happened to us in the biblical past. It is a moral truth about the society we're living in right now. We cannot separate ourselves from it, nor confess it away, nor blame somebody else. But our conscience instructs us to take responsibility for the sin woven into our world and our lives.

Our conscience in relation to those with dementia must encompass more than individual sins we have committed against individual people with dementia. Most of us have not abused or stolen from elderly relatives whose cognitive impairments prevent them from protecting themselves. Our conscience asks us what good we have done, not just individually but collectively, for vulnerable people with dementia. Our conscience asks us whose side we're on.

Have we advocated for better dementia care in our health system? Have we told our politicians we would pay higher taxes to ensure truly effective and adequate care? Why shouldn't your parish, your school, your prayer group make that appeal – not just to the minister of health but to the minister of finance? Not just to your senator and congressional representative in Washington, but to your fellow citizens? Can't you write a letter to the editor? Can't you tweet on behalf of better dementia care? Whose side is your parish on? Whose side are you on?

**Confidence** eludes most of us. If we have any at all, it comes at us in giant bubbles that burst on contact. Confidence in what? Not ourselves, certainly. If confidence is centred on ourselves then it is not about caring, because caring is about how we relate to other people.

But what if we are confident that caring for people with dementia will make a difference in their lives? What if we are confident that this effort is not useless or unimportant? What if we are confident that every small action taken on behalf of those with dementia is necessary?

**Commitment** is easy for a faith community. Faith communities exist to be committed. Otherwise, what's the Creed for?

If we believe in the Holy Spirit, the holy catholic church, the communion of saints, the forgiveness of sins, the resurrection of the body and life everlasting, do we therefore believe in those parishioners who walk in fear, struggle to speak, tremble in the grip of Parkinson's? Are we committed to them?

**Creativity** frankly scares us. It seems to be the property of some special class of people – artists, dancers, poets, architects, etc. Most of us feel unqualified to be creative.

But the word is not primarily about startling originality and art. It's about what we make and how we make it. Making dinner, making conversation, making tea are not necessarily original or artistic accomplishments, but they are creative. They contribute something concrete to the world we live in and how we live in it.

A creative response to dementia in the community is not necessarily the invention of anything new. The creative response simply acknowledges and acts on the need as directly and concretely as possible. It places care somewhere that care is needed. Are people cut off and lonely? Then talk to them. Are people lost? Then guide them. Are people afraid? Reassure and accompany them.

A parish determined to respond to dementia needs to ask, "What do people with dementia need?" It can then respond to that need concretely. That's creativity. It is also care.

# Real Planning

## How to begin acknowledging parishioners with dementia

If a parish is going to actively include people with dementia in its community, it will need a plan. The plan will not emerge from this book (though I hope the book will help) or from a memo from the archdiocese or even from the fertile imagination of the parish's talented pastor. There has to be a process. The plan has to fit your particular parish, its capabilities, its concerns and its prayers.

Some mechanism of election and selection must choose a few hopeful, sensible people willing to come together and discuss the parish's dementia plans. They must consider

- the scope of the challenge
- how people with dementia right now participate (or don't) in our rites and sacraments, especially eucharist, confession, anointing of the sick, weddings, baptisms and funerals
- how the parish already welcomes the cognitively impaired
- where and how the parish fails to welcome
- dementia-specific physical barriers in the church building
- what the parish does for people who can't come to church, who live in area nursing homes, hospitals and in their own homes.

Imagine some similar committee brought together to consider the parish's efforts in marriage preparation or youth ministry. Would such a committee get very far before deciding to talk to the people it aims to serve? I hope not.

There may be some hesitation about asking for direction from people who can't always remember who you are or why you called on them. It may seem quite rude to confront your elders with their decline and their limitations. But your committee will not know how to serve people it doesn't know. It will not know what these people want without asking them.

Do not call parishioners with dementia to a meeting. Don't summon them to the church hall. A crowd or even a gaggle of people asking a long series of questions can be frightening and confusing for people who often struggle with hearing and have trouble following the thread of a complex conversation. These people feel vulnerable and exposed when they go to the grocery store or the bank. They don't like crowds. They know they need help, and when out of their homes they are not confident they will get it. They've reached a point in their lives where everyone seems strange. What could be worse than a meeting with a lot of strangers? Any encounter with their own parish should be a more positive, less frightening, less vexing experience.

Gather information one on one. Meet people in their homes, even if those homes are nursing homes or hospital wards. Send one person to visit. This visitor should not sit back with a clipboard reading off prepared questions and writing down answers. Leave that to the health care and social work professionals. The interviewer's job is first, foremost and almost entirely to establish a bond of mutual trust, empathy and friendship – something we Catholics call communion. Bring a coffee or a cup of tea with you and maybe a treat the two of you can share. If the parishioner lives with family, or depends on friends who live next door, include them in the visit. Talk about the weather, the Blue Jays (not the Astros), mutual friends. The conversation will eventually wind its way round to the parish and dementia.

While small talk continues, notice your fellow parishioner's environment. What is their apartment or house like? Clean and tidy or dangerously accumulating junk, newspapers and the detritus of living day to day? Is there a computer? Is the television on? At what volume? When the fridge door opens, what do you see? Has she dressed up for your visit or did she forget you were coming? Is there a walking cane, a walker or a wheelchair you haven't seen before?

As you notice these things, you are not diagnosing her dementia or planning an intervention. You are neither qualified nor authorized to interfere in this person's life. But what kind of friend would not notice?

The core question, the place where this conversation must end up, is "What can the parish do for you?"

"I would like there to be somebody who would phone me, maybe even every day," Janet Somerville told me.

Somerville is one of the most remarkable contributors to Canadian Catholic life through the late 20th century. She was one of the first lay women to study theology full-time at the University of St. Michael's College graduate faculty of theology. She was present in Rome for parts of the Second Vatican Council. As a young woman, she prayed the office with members of The Grail. She was one of the founders and eventually a long-time editor of *The Catholic New Times* in Toronto. She was the first Catholic to be the general secretary of the Canadian Council of Churches. She has been called upon by individual bishops and by the Canadian Conference of Catholic Bishops for advice. She wrote and spoke on behalf of the Jesuit Forum for Social Faith and Justice, helping to produce study guides to papal encyclicals. She was awarded the Order of Canada.

But Somerville is past 80 now. Her doctors have spoken to her about her declining memory. Given her mother's descent into severe dementia, she's not surprised that both she and her doctors have noticed this change.

A while ago she came back from a visit with a friend, down the hall from her apartment, to find her bookcase on fire. She had left a candle burning before nipping just a few doors down. The visit lasted longer than she intended. On her return, faced with a small blaze, she called 911 and then somehow put it out before the fire trucks arrived.

She was embarrassed by all the fuss, but also afraid.

"Burning the place down is one thing that I imagine in my dark moments," she told me.

Somerville has been a member of Our Lady of Lourdes parish in downtown Toronto most of her life. She is well known to parishioners and the pastoral staff. She knows she is lucky in that she can count on her parish.

"There would be so many people (at Lourdes) who would take it for granted that being that close to someone in their decline was a normal part of parish life," she told me.

Being able to count on the unorganized, unplanned goodwill of her parish is a blessing – but it's not the same as a pastoral plan designed to help her and people like her. That's why she wants phone calls.

"I think Lourdes is spiritually and psychologically ready. I don't know if it has strategies prepared," Somerville said.

For her, the simple strategy she asks for is a buddy system to ensure phone calls.

"Certainly on Saturday sometime, and then on Sunday," she said. "This person would know what Mass I was going to try and make. And this person would phone on Saturdays to let me know tomorrow is Sunday. Because which day of the week it is is one of the first things to go. It would be wonderful if that person would phone me on Sunday and say, 'I will be round in half an hour to walk to church with you.' That would be great."

Somerville wants to be as much a part of her parish as she can be, and for as long as she can. That doesn't necessarily mean she's going to serve on committees, proclaim the first or second readings at Mass or direct traffic in the parking lot.

"One of the things you have to face when you hit my age is you can't rejoice in being useful anymore," she said.

But she can imagine herself praying for and with her parish. If someone were to hand her next Sunday morning's petitioning prayers on a weekday, she would pray them with gusto. Should there be particular concerns in the parish, or particular parishioners facing difficulty, she would pray for them by name.

Though I've known her 20 years, Somerville may one day forget my name. Even her associations with my face may fade, or become mingled with other people. Or this may never happen. But if it does, both she and I hope to accept it in the context of gratitude for her life. But Somerville believes, and I concur, that she will never forget how to pray.

Even liturgical prayer, rites and ceremonies are not easily erased, Jesuit gerontologist Fr. John Siberski told me.

"For the person who has been observant and participates, they can maintain a very complete memory or memory traces, particularly of repetitive things such as liturgy, the prayers," he said. "One of the Jesuits at Campion Centre (a long-term care facility for Jesuits just outside Boston) told me about his uncle who was practically mute. But if you put a rosary in his hand and began with 'I believe in God...' he could run through the entire thing without missing a beat."

For Somerville, it goes deeper than whatever prayers she may be able to recite a few years from now. She knows her memory will cling to God.

"I'm not afraid of forgetting the words of prayers. Because words are ambiguous anyway," she said. "The fact of God and the fact that God loves the whole creation and also loves me is so much the centre of my hope that God forgetting me, or me forgetting God, is unthinkable. It's unimaginable."

The entire point of a parish strategy for dementia would be to back her bet.

# Reality Out There

## Where to find those who need you most

The people at Mass on Sunday who struggle with memory and speech are just the tip of the dementia iceberg. A parish dementia strategy is not complete if it's all about what happens inside the church.

Dementia is an illness – a very severe, life-limiting illness. If the parish cares about people with dementia, it's more likely to find them in hospitals and nursing homes than in the church nave and sanctuary. The Canadian Institute for Health Information found that in 2015–2016, 69 percent of Canada's long-term care home residents had some form of dementia. Add in those who have had a stroke or some other form of trauma causing cognitive impairment and you're up to 87 percent of long-term care residents.[37]

As health policy has focused on moving people out of expensive hospital beds whenever they can be better cared for in another, cheaper setting, the percentage of patients with dementia in long-term care facilities has increased. Those 2015–2016 numbers are probably low compared with our present reality.

In the U.S., where Medicaid is the only public program that pays for residential care of people with dementia, 42 percent of residents in nursing homes have some form of dementia.[38]

To care for people with dementia, Catholics have to do precisely what Pope Francis has been asking for since he was elected – get out of the choir loft, exit the sacristy and venture into the street. "I prefer a Church which is bruised, hurting and dirty because it has been out on the streets, rather than a Church which is unhealthy from being confined and from clinging to its own security," the pope wrote in *Evangelii Gaudium* (49).

A parish that cares about dementia ought to be an ideal pool of volunteers for the local nursing home.

Most parishes already have a hospital visitation ministry. Some of these are conceived of purely in terms of getting the eucharist out to people who can't come to church. I'm not suggesting this means automatons sent out to hospitals and nursing homes with a ciborium, incapable of anything but holding up a host and repeating "The body of Christ" over and over. But if the parish volunteer has been primed to deliver communion, then any conversation or time spent with people is extra. Once communion has been delivered, it's time to move on.

The entire purpose of a visitation ministry to nursing home residents with dementia begins and ends with conversation, touch, music and time spent together. No one would deny sacramental communion to the sick, or put it in second place. But unless there is another, separate ministry of visitation, then that communion wafer reaches residents in a vacuum. Without the context of relationships, without the context of a wider community, the real presence has been confined to a narrow channel.

The real presence of Christ is there in the consecrated bread and wine, certainly. But it is also present in the community, in whose name this sacrifice is offered on the altar.[39] Include these nursing home patients in the community and you have included them in the body of Christ. But can you include them if you spend no time with them?

Is it meaningful to spend time with people who don't remember who you are and won't remember you next week either?

"In those fleeting moments, when there is the clarity of someone there speaking, yes," Providence Hospital – Houses of Providence operations leader for volunteer services Faye Robinson told me. "I still think the human spirit requires acknowledgement. I still believe it wholly requires touch."

With 288 residents in Toronto's Houses of Providence long-term care home, it requires dozens of volunteers to be there over the course of a week – to daily acknowledge the life and humanity of people left lonely by dementia and the passage of time. During the COVID-19 crisis, lockdowns expelled the volunteers from the Houses of Providence for months. Robinson and the clinical staff at Providence saw the real damage that sort of isolation did to patients. They saw accelerated deterioration among residents when the volunteers were absent, even though volunteers are not involved in medical care.

"Volunteers do all the little things that feed the soul," Robinson said. "The more that brain, that mind, is engaged, we know that people are happier. But the (medical) staff don't have the time to do it."

We don't have to have dementia to know the pain of loneliness. Loneliness is epidemic in our society. In the United Kingdom, it has been recognized as a health emergency, and a cabinet minister has been put in charge of a government-wide strategy to tackle loneliness.[40] Why would we assume loneliness is any less distressing, less damaging, for people with dementia?

Dementia itself cuts people off. It makes conversations first difficult and then impossible. It leaves people fearful of strangers and of crowds. But there are other sources of loneliness.

"We serve specifically a geriatric population," explained Roberts. "Their spouses die, their friends die and there's a deep-seated loneliness that really feeds depression and other ailments. Having volunteers there to have a conversation with them, to laugh out loud with them – that companionship goes a long way …. We all have a need for companionship. As we get older, there's a loneliness that sets in."

Visiting dementia patients in a long-term care home or hospital isn't for everyone.

"There are people who haven't had experience with family members who have had dementia," Roberts said. "Do they have the fortitude to go into that space and see someone screaming at the wall after seeing a plant and calling it a spider, and (shouting) 'Do something about it – kill the spider!'"

The good news for a parish is that they don't have to vet or train volunteers who do take this on. That's Robinson's job. Most health care institutions will have someone or some process to manage volunteers. The parish is free to encourage people to give it a try.

"This is something that needs to appeal to you as a sense of duty," said Robinson. "If you have a heart for it in particular – if you feel your purpose is to help others in this environment."

Robinson wants Providence volunteers to be happy. She knows volunteers are happiest if they know why they're there. She wants them to feel like they belong.

"We try to get a square peg into a square hole, rather than force somebody into a role they couldn't possibly manage," she said. "We offer training in dementia. We give them a sense of what they might in fact walk into. That really helps."

Robinson is clear with all her volunteers that they're not there to take on medical roles.

"Why are you here?" she asks. "Are you here to diagnose?"

She trains volunteers to assist with feeding, but not for patients with dysphagia or who are at risk of choking. She hammers home with staff and volunteers that no volunteer should do anything the volunteer feels would endanger them or the patient in any way, even a little bit.

"Most of them, if they were uncomfortable with a task, would say (to staff), 'No, call Faye,'" she said.

She also tells her volunteers to be selfish. She wants them to get something out of the time they spend at Providence.

"Volunteering can be a selfish endeavour, but in a very good way," she said. "Because it really feeds one's soul. It helps you grow as a human being."

# The Architecture of Reality

## Getting your building dementia-ready

That little group of hopeful and sensible people called together to review how the parish welcomes and includes parishioners with dementia should spend some of its time and energy talking about the building and its surroundings.

Thanks to COVID-19, most of us have spent some part of 2020 and 2021 unable to go to church. Though Catholics are generally taught in time for first communion that church is not just a building, being banned from the building during this time has been painful. But, thinking beyond COVID, what if that building itself has the effect of banning parishioners with dementia?

Whether your church is 20 or 200 years old, there is almost no chance the original architects, or any of the long succession of pastors and renovators who followed, have ever thought much about how that building works for people with cognitive impairments. As we fill our churches up with votive candles, statues and paintings; as we throw down mats to absorb snow melting off our boots, or install speakers and microphones, renovate the bathrooms, reconfigure the kitchen and dining area for coffee after Mass, repave the parking lot, etc., we're not thinking about the parishioner who sometimes gets lost, who fears tripping and falling, or forgets where they were going, or becomes confused.

We know the effect bad architecture and bad interior design has on us. We've all been in buildings that leave us anxious and disoriented. Who hasn't wished they could throttle an architect while wandering confusing passageways, trying locked doors, looking for the bathroom? People with dementia have these experiences as well, but for them they are more distressing and harder to overcome.

It is to be hoped that no parish churches were designed by bad architects who forgot to draw bathrooms into their design until a week before deadline, then stuck them into a corner just past the furnace room. We all hope that as old churches evolve, builders don't add stairs between the worship space and every other part of the building – then more stairs between those parts of the building until a zip line would be more useful than a walker on the way from the pew to the parking lot. God save us from cheapo sound systems that leave dead spots where nothing is audible, in contrast to the pews underneath the speakers where every word is shouted. Have you ever noticed pews arranged so close together that getting in and out, past that pew guardian who insists on sitting at the end of an empty row, would challenge the corps du ballet? Such pews aren't just a problem for people with dementia.

Reviewing the building for impediments to the cognitively impaired won't benefit only the parishioners with dementia.

Often, we're just stuck with the building we have. There's no pretending that reconfiguring old churches to make them more accessible doesn't cost money. The financial challenges for many parishes are great. But those challenges should raise deeper questions about our priorities. If we're not spending money to make the parish safe and accessible for everyone, then what do we spend our money on?

In 1991, Pope St. John Paul II tried to have us all think seriously about what is meant by a "preferential option for the poor."

"Different forms of poverty are being experienced by groups which live on the margins of society, by the elderly and the sick, by the victims of consumerism, and even more immediately by so many refugees and migrants," the pope wrote in *Centesimus Annus*, his summation of Catholic social teaching 100 years after Pope Leo XIII's *Rerum Novarum*.

When we find the weak, the vulnerable and the suffering among us, whatever the source of their troubles, it is to them we must go first. They should get our attention, our sympathy and our money.

Of course, spending money we don't have is difficult. But not all changes to make a church more accessible will require a second mortgage. Signage, moving furniture out of the way, turning on the lights you already have, propping open heavy doors – any of these measures and many more might make the church easier to navigate.

The process of paying attention to how parishioners with dementia experience their church should begin with expert opinion. Invite someone from the local Alzheimer's society to walk through the building with you. If you don't know where to find them, call the Alzheimer's Society of Canada at 1-800-616-8816. They'll give you a name and a phone number. In the U.S., your state chapter of the Alzheimer's Association (alz.org) can hook you up with a faith ambassador.

At the walk-through, bring along a clipboard and a pen. Take notes.

If you are a suburban or rural parish, start in the parking lot. If you're downtown, assemble on the sidewalk. Imagine you are arriving at church in whatever way people normally do.

Imagine also that you have difficulties with memory and concentration. People with dementia find it harder and harder to remember where they were going or why they came there in the first place. Can you remind them with signs? Are whatever signs already exist at eye level – not your eye level but the eye level of an older person who walks with a cane or walker? Are the signs readable – in bright, contrasting and large letters? Such signs should eschew cute or abstract icons. Playing card jacks and queens or cowgirls and cowboys on the door of men's and women's washrooms are not helpful to people in even the earliest stages of dementia. Just say it in English or the dominant language of the parish: "Men's toilet" or "Women's toilet."

Signage is a consideration even outside the church. Traditional church architecture with steeples and crosses and stained glass is certainly helpful, but not necessarily sufficient. Are there signs in front of the church and in the parking lot to signal to people that they have arrived at church?

Inside the building, pictures can help. Pictures of food in the dining area or pictures of groups of people talking in a meeting room – anything to remind people of what normally goes on in a particular room and to distinguish these rooms from the main worship space.

As dementia progresses, people have more and more trouble processing and interpreting visual information. As we get older, we all experience hearing loss, but dementia can make it more difficult to guess at the meaning of words half-heard. Proper lighting and sound systems can make an enormous difference for these parishioners.

An area in shadow can cause confusion. High contrast between pools of light and surrounding dark areas can make it difficult for people with dementia to see or understand any of the details in either of these dark or light areas. Under dramatically contrasting lighting, they may not perceive the pew, the kneeler, the confessional or the steps leading up to the altar. What may seem to us a softly lit sacred space will appear to them a dark, empty and scary place. Attempts to navigate such spaces will result in trips and falls.

A snow mat seems practical. But for the elderly, both with dementia and without, it's a tripping hazard. That polished, highly reflective floor intended to mimic marble (or perhaps it is marble) looks slippery or wet to people with dementia. Contrasting floor colours can appear to be barriers, or might look like a step up or down from where a person is currently standing.

If you've got marble floors, you probably shouldn't rip them up. If you've got old carpet, you probably should rip it up. If the parish is shopping for new flooring or carpet, avoid strong, contrasting patterns that can cause problems for people with dementia. Look for something plain or lightly mottled.

The best solutions to such problems, however, are not technical or architectural or expensive. They are people. Call them welcomers or ushers or helpers or ministers of hospitality or whatever you will. They are volunteers. Put them at the door 20 minutes before Mass and have them watch for anybody who might have trouble. It should seem normal to have someone there to guide parishioners to an empty pew, to ask others to make room for them, to settle them in comfortably and hand them a bulletin.

The welcomers simply need to be on hand should any difficulty arise from the time a parishioner arrives at church until they leave. A sign pointing the way to the washrooms is good. A friendly face who can accompany a parishioner there and back is better.

Running water in a centrally placed baptismal font is undoubtedly a beautiful symbol of faith in Christ as the source of life. But parishioners with dementia haven't just experienced hearing loss. Changes in the brain have changed how they process sounds and attach meaning to those sounds. Running water in the baptismal font now muffles or blocks all the high-frequency sounds. Its babbling and splashing confuses itself with the consonants of the priest preaching a homily or the lector reading St. Paul's letter to the Romans. These problems of perception may affect many parishioners with hearing loss. For those with dementia, the sound of running water, especially if they cannot locate its source or understand the reason for it, may convey a sense that something bad is about to happen.

Old sound systems, many of them badly installed or poorly understood by those with keys to the control panel, have likely driven more Catholics away from the church than all the communist revolutions of the 20th century combined. But the problem isn't necessarily the technology, voice coach David Smukler told me.

"We're always working with the acoustical problems," he said. "The more stone, the more metal, the more ineffective the communication is …. It's about understanding the acoustical nature of the room. Then, if it's necessary to use a mic, there are so many modern, good mics that are so simple, that can be pinned on. But people play with the buttons."

Knowing how to use the microphones and the mixing board will obviously help and won't cost anything. Again, find a volunteer – somebody whose job is to operate the mixing board during Mass. Don't just set it and forget it. Different presiders sound different. The choir will fill the worship space with varying effectiveness depending on what it's singing, who is singing and how tightly packed the church is. Lectors will have varying ability to project their voices as they proclaim the readings. Somebody with some minimal training on the soundboard can move a slider or two to compensate for many of these problems.

If there are dead spots right next to areas with good reverberation, then simple sound baffles might help. Nothing will help as much as training priests and lectors to project their voices. Try putting somebody in a red sweater in the middle of the church and telling the presider, readers and cantor to direct their words to that person. If they can do that, you may find the microphones work just fine.

"The human training is not a major expense, but it takes time," Smukler said. "When it comes to the acoustical work, it depends on the sanctuary. Some can be solved fairly easily."

To include people with dementia in the liturgy is obviously important. But our responsibility does not end there. We cannot abandon them as we gather for coffee after Mass. We cannot exclude them from our meetings and prayer groups, committees and projects.

Outside the nave and sanctuary, are parishioners faced with long hallways? Is it clear where these hallways lead? Is the parish hall named after some beloved, long-dead pastor? Are you really so sure that when people are told to gather in Fr. Doyle Hall or the Sr. Elizabeth Shoemaker room that they have any idea where that is or who you're talking about? Does that sign on the door of the "St. Cecilia Room" mean anything to a parishioner who is perhaps a little confused about where she's going? Does the parish have a room with a name like the "Isaac Hecker Auditorium," but everyone calls it "The Big Room"? Confusing, perhaps?

People with dementia don't just have cognitive problems. They often find a walk down the hallway exhausting. If it can be done safely, why not put a couple of inviting, comfortable chairs in an alcove along the way – places where people can stop with a friend or a stranger to rest and chat.

Inside the washroom, or at the sink in the kitchen, are hot and cold taps clearly marked?

Cluttered spaces aren't just dangerous for people with dementia, presenting tripping risks or impossible obstacles for walkers and wheelchairs. Clutter sows confusion. Catholics need not become Quakers to accommodate the cognitively impaired. Catholic churches and Catholic culture demand statues and paintings and decoration and stations of the cross and side chapels and stained glass and holy water fonts – the whole shebang. But none of this needs to crowd into clear pathways that lead people where they want and need to go.

Walk those pathways to the pew, to the altar, to the confessional and to the parish hall. Walk these routes through your church gripping onto a walker as if you depended on it to keep you upright. Do it during the mad rush to the parking lot just after Mass and see how far you get before you are overwhelmed by obstacles and distractions.

This building embodies so much of who we are. It contains our history and our hope for the future, from the saints in the stained glass to the baptismal font. We should not allow who we are to become an obstacle course or an assault on the equanimity of those among us with dementia.

# Real Liturgy

## The source and summit of caring

"Take this, all of you …. Do this in memory of me." The central event, the source and summit of the life of the church, is an act of memory. We offer up our memory of God and ask in return for God to remember us. "Remember, Lord, your Church …."[41]

Jesus' instruction at the last supper is to "all of you." The Mass is not the possession of the presider or the act of any one person. We remember together – a collective memory.

"That's the whole point of anamnesis," Jesuit Fr. Gilles Mongeau, author of *Embracing Wisdom: The Summa Theologiae and Spiritual Pedagogy*,[42] told me. "The body of Christ has a memory – which is partly scripture, but it's also simply the repeated living out of the ritual. It's the proclamation of the Word. It's all of these things that are acts of memory, acts of common memory."

We cannot, must not, exclude from this memory the dead. Our fathers and mothers, grandfathers and grandmothers, passed this irreplaceable cargo of memory along a vast chain through generations. We can't forget them. Much less can we exclude those still with us.

"There's lots and lots of biblical concern about memory," Mongeau explained. "God needs to remember us. We need to remember God. So there's lots of biblical warrant for being concerned about memory."

Even if a lifetime of memories have abandoned parishioners with dementia, we must not abandon them. The more they have lost their own personal ability to remember, the greater our responsibility to hang on to our collective shared memory for their sake.

We hold this memory of the feast and sacrifice of the Mass in trust for them. If the sacrament itself is a mystery, so is the persistence of their memories of it – even when they have forgotten their own children's names. What these parishioners remember as they pray through the Mass is more than the words of prayers. Even when they have forgotten liturgical words and actions, in the midst of ancient rites they remember who they are as they find themselves in prayer.

"I saw it with my own dad, my father," palliative care chaplain David Rebelo told me. "I mean, he insisted on going to church every day when he started to have dementia and it developed into Alzheimer's. The traditional prayers, like the rosary… the Our Father, Hail Mary – all those things – they're almost primal, almost innate. I think it's something that's instilled in them."

Working in palliative care at Providence Hospital in Toronto, Rebelo witnesses the miracle of memory every day. He also knows how the invocation and exercise of whatever memories remain can heal, even if that healing must be repeated hour by hour and day by day.

He told me about one of his patients. "She said to me, I feel abandoned by God."

This woman had prayed the Magnificat, the Our Father and the Hail Mary all her life. Even as she struggled to remember where she was and why she was there, she still knew these prayers.[43]

"I have to be there almost daily to pray with her and remind her, 'No, God is here,' Rebelo said. "You could see it in her face. Her face just calms down."

Deacon Matt Dineen has seen his wife, who has a severe and rare form of frontotemporal dementia, become a little more herself at Mass.

"She's almost non-verbal now," Dineen told me. "But the songs, the recitation of the Lord's Prayer – I know for a fact that she's in familiar (territory). She may not be able to name the parish, but she is somewhere where she knows it's her second home. It's a familiar setting and one that's important."

So does your parish need a special dementia-friendly Mass? This Mass might be shorter than other Sunday Masses; more like a half-hour weekday Mass. It might feature a shorter and simpler homily. The music at this Mass might be geared to parishioners who remember hymns and chants from 50 or 60 years ago. The priest presiding at this Mass could cultivate a slow, carefully enunciated style of speaking. Priests, lectors, deacons, cantors, ushers, ministers of holy communion – anyone with a defined role – should be prepared for interruptions, odd behaviour and people who need assistance.

Jesuit gerontologist Fr. John Siberski has a friend who cares for her mother, bringing her to Mass on Sundays. The mother is of a generation that never saw the chalice offered to the assembly. Her parish is now a place that does this regularly. Usually, the daughter, following behind, would nudge her mother into the line for reception of the host and then back to her pew. Once, however, the eucharistic minister with the cup was standing a little closer than usual, holding the chalice about belt high.

"Mom saw the golden bowl with liquid," said Siberski. "She dipped her fingers and blessed herself and kept going."

Such missteps do not mean the Catholic with dementia is simply lost, dazed and confused at Mass.

"Most of the time, people – even the ones who are severely demented – still get it," Siberski said of his own experience celebrating Mass at nursing homes. "They still follow along. They still know the prayers. It goes great … It's an opportunity to engage in that which is familiar, well-known and loved."

While the persistence of liturgical memory – the ability to say the prayers, make the sign of the cross, follow along – is often a wonder, absolutely nothing depends on our ability to come up with the right words or understand precisely what the priest is saying. The Mass and all of the sacraments are sovereign acts of God. They do not require our permission or our penetrating insights. They do not depend on the worthiness of the priest, the uprightness of the bishop or anyone else. They are not contingent on anything but the free choice of an incarnate, loving God. So how could we dare to make participation in the sacrament dependent on the progress of this disease? How do we dare say there's no point in bringing Mum to Mass?

There's nothing wrong with special dementia-friendly Masses, particularly if they fill a pastoral need. But they are not absolutely necessary. Even if a dementia-friendly Mass is scheduled, parishioners with dementia and mild cognitive impairment will continue to attend the Mass they've always attended. That routine is important to them, as are all experiences of the familiar.

"When she's home, she can look out the window and receive the confirmation of who she is by seeing the clothesline, or her neighbour's swing on the back porch," said Siberski.

Her regular Mass at the regular time and with people she has known for many years can also confirm for her who she is.

"If your mom has been going to Catholic Mass all her life, this is not the time to take her to a Presbyterian church because it's more convenient," Siberski said. "Familiarity with the liturgy allows us to confirm for ourselves, even though we can't articulate it, who we are and what we're about."

So at that regular Sunday morning Mass, the parish needs to welcome people with dementia by not asking them to be extra vulnerable or to do difficult, challenging things just to get through it. Don't make them manoeuvre a walker out of their pew and into the central aisle for communion. Don't make them stand there wobbling, balancing their cane on one wrist while trying to receive communion in the other hand, bringing it to their mouth and making the sign of the cross before they can safely reposition the cane on the floor to begin the walk back to the pew. There is little chance this whole scenario is going to go without a hitch week after week. At some point the minister of holy communion will end up lifting either the Body of Christ, the body of the parishioner or both up off the floor.

An unobstructed pew at the front of the church where the priest or the minister of holy communion can easily find parishioners with disabilities and bring them communion, before serving those in the communion line, is half the solution. The other half is well-trained ushers or welcomers who direct these parishioners to the reserved front-row pew as they arrive.

Mass is not the only liturgy in Catholic life. Particularly for an older generation, regular confession is also how they have lived their lives in the church. Should we take that away from them? Should people with dementia go to confession? Do they need to go to confession?

"Some (priests) will get all huffy and say, 'Oh no, they can't sin,'" said Siberski.

Going to confession was never a measure of how much we sin. It's not a guard rail we raise higher given a greater potential for sin. The sacrament isn't about sin, but about forgiveness, healing, reconciliation. The starting point is, undoubtedly, to know ourselves in specific and concrete ways to be sinners. The church is full of sinners. It exists for us sinners and is run by sinners. That's why the arc of this liturgy of reconciliation bends to forgiveness – always, every time. Why would we expel people with dementia from this oasis of God's forgiveness? Why would we expel them from the church's great communion of sinners?

"But it's helpful for the priest to know ahead of time," Siberski said.

Siberski has heard many confessions from elderly people with dementia. When he was fairly new in the priesthood, he heard an afternoon's worth of confessions across three generations in one family.

"Being in the confessional, a woman came in and she said, 'Father, before I begin, my mother's coming next and she has Alzheimer's.' Then she began her confession," recalled Siberski. "Then the door opened and the door closed and there was silence at the other end of the screen. I said, 'You can begin,' and she had no clue. So I began, 'Bless me, Father.' Then she went right through the confession. But then she left, halfway through the absolution. Then it got really funny, because the door opened and closed again. I said, 'You can begin now.' I hear this nine-year-old voice say, 'I forgot how.' I think it was her great-grandson. I almost lost it."

I was once a volunteer at a nursing home in Saint Paul, Minnesota. In those glorious days of hot dishes and Jell-O salad, I became friends with a man at the nursing home who went through days of laughter and mischief followed by days of terror and gloom. Sometimes his fear of death was so overwhelming, he would sit up in his bed and wail. He knew he was about to die and he would grip my arm and ask me to find him a priest.

The nurses had rather a better handle on his actual physical condition than he did. If I could loosen his grip and make my way down the hall, they would tell me, "He's not going to die." They advised against bothering the priest for the 15th or 16th time that year.

Whether or not the cause was real, his fear was palpable. So I found a Jesuit friend who came with his little leather bag and a stole. The effect of holy oil, confession and communion over the course of a 15-minute visit to his bedside was so dramatic, I thought I was witnessing a miracle. He was comfortably asleep 10 minutes after the priest left his side. My older and wiser Jesuit friend informed me it was not a miracle, just the sacrament of the sick. It happens all the time.

It happens if the patient can get the sacrament – if there are priests available, if there are volunteers who can call those priests on their behalf. The nurses who thought their patient should be actually dying before bothering the priest mistook this sacrament of healing. It is not some magic applied as our last breath escapes. It restores us to our selves – that true self discovered first in baptism.

The dementia-ready parish must make the sacrament of the sick available as widely and frequently as possible. There will never be enough priests, of course. Healing Masses can help, at least for those not confined to nursing home beds.

Ritual, the words that connect us to each other and to God, the ways in which we offer ourselves in response to God's love – these are our birthright. Your parish's dementia committee is not looking for ways to control liturgical life, or make it more efficient, or fulfill the requirements of a contract with the diocese – as if your parish were a spiritual fast-food franchise. The liturgical life of the parish is a gift to be shared. Whenever the parishioner with dementia is included, then that gift is truly given and received by all. This is how your parish can be really present to those who feel the absence of the world they once knew.

# Physical Reality

## Health is our collective concern

That DNA sequence in your cells is holding onto secrets. The greatest scientific enterprise of our time has been to listen for the many ways this vast yet microscopic spiral of DNA, distributed throughout your body in skin cells, brain cells, blood cells and more, has been whispering its secrets.

If you have two copies of the APOE4 gene, your chances of developing Alzheimer's are eight to 12 times the chances for people who have different versions of APOE, or only one copy of APOE4. But we don't know why that is or how it works.[44]

At the same time as science has discovered this genetic link, researchers have also shown that most forms of dementia are not simply genetic. If your mother or father or both had a form of dementia, it doesn't mean you also will get it. Almost every case of Alzheimer's represents a genetically sporadic occurrence. It does not run in families.[45] Inherited or familial cases of Alzheimer's disease account for 2 to 5 percent of all cases.

Knowing that risks for the disease can be read genetically tells us non-scientists that dementia is not merely a malfunction in the brain. It is a disease that can be found in every cell of your body. Dementia has origins in the entire physical system of our being.

The disease also has causes that begin long before we notice a cognitive decline. Thus, the first way to care for people with dementia is to prevent it. A pastoral plan for dementia must include a parish plan to encourage and support brain health.

We are not the helpless victims of whatever chemistry is going on inside our skulls. If the disease is connected to physical health, we can do something about that. As a community of people who care about and for each other, a parish can guide people to step around the physical threats to our cognitive health.

My sister, Susan Swan, is a nurse practitioner who coordinates and directs home care for geriatric patients in the suburbs west of Toronto. She calls Alzheimer's "type 3 diabetes." The risk diabetes poses to our brain health is not subtle. Those of us with type 2 diabetes are twice as likely as the rest of us to develop dementia. Even if Alzheimer's is not classed as a form of diabetes in medical textbooks, the link between the two diseases is more than statistical.

If more than three million Canadians and 34 million Americans (about one in every 10 North Americans) have type 2 diabetes,[46][47] is that any concern of your parish dementia committee?

Diabetes was a concern for Jesuit Fr. Michael Stogre when he was director of the Anishinabe Spiritual Centre on Anderson Lake, in Northern Ontario, between 1990 and 2012.

Stogre was the kind of Jesuit who wasn't satisfied with a B.A. in classics, an M.A. and licentiate in philosophy and, of course, a Master of Divinity. After his ordination in 1974, he found his way to medical school. His MD and licence to practise became useful tools in the Jesuit struggle on behalf of people in a then-poor neighbourhood of Toronto and among the neglected and abused Indigenous people of Northern Ontario.

At the Anishinabe Spiritual Centre, where Jesuits trained a generation of Indigenous elders to be deacons and sought to help the church become an ally of Indigenous Canadians, Stogre believed Jesuits and Indigenous people could together build better communities. But looking at the situation in front of him, Stogre saw an epidemic of diabetes that crippled Indigenous communities on Manitoulin Island and throughout Northern Ontario.

He teamed up with nurse and community leader Rosella Kenoshameg to lead a proper epidemiological study and to begin advocating with provincial and local health authorities for diabetes education and programming. He brought people together to talk about their diabetes, to learn from one another, to support one another and to advocate for lifestyle changes.

Stogre saw that this amounted to much more than just preaching diet and regular exercise. He brought people together at the Anishinabe Spiritual Centre, where they came to understand all that diabetes was and meant in their lives. It was knowledge they owned because it wasn't a lecture visited on them from on high. People talked to one another about their diabetes, and how they had become so sedentary, and how their eating habits were formed. They recalled growing up institutionalized at residential schools where the life skills their parents knew – cooking, hunting, living off the land – were crushed.

As they talked, these elders who struggled with diabetes turned away from passive fatalism. They would not simply accept that this disease or our colonial history had rendered them, their children and their communities bystanders in the world. They learned to actively live and value their own lives, build their communities and take pride in themselves.

Improvements in diet and exercise naturally followed, and as people brought their diabetes under control, Stogre witnessed how they also took control of their lives.

The Jesuits' historic ministry among the people of the Three Fires Confederacy (Odawa, Ojibwa and Potawatomi) reaches back into the 17th century. The relationship isn't exactly a parish, though it now includes three parishes on Manitoulin Island plus the Anishinabe Spiritual Centre. It is a work of accompaniment and a conscious encounter between the church (with all of its history, good and bad) and a culture.

The relationships Stogre came to value weren't medical, technical or scientific. They were pastoral. He would listen to people, hope with them, pray with them, encourage them. He let his medical licence lapse, but he was still helping people live lives as free of diabetes as they could be.

High cholesterol, high blood pressure, depression, high alcohol consumption, head injuries, hearing loss, obesity and sedentary lifestyles, smoking, colourless diets full of starch, salt and processed foods, loneliness, a history of non-engagement in school followed by dropping out, bad sleep habits, even living next to a busy highway have all been statistically linked to higher rates of dementia. If Oprah can't solve all these problems, does your parish stand a chance?

The parish probably can't and shouldn't hector every parishioner into a dull, stoic, abstemious, irreproachable lifestyle. Any church aiming to play the part of nanny to its parishioners is bound for the lonely oblivion that awaits old nannies. But parishes can give people opportunities to make changes they themselves wish to make. The parish could bring people together to examine their health and lifestyles.

Couldn't your hopeful, sensible dementia committee organize cooking classes to get people eating better? What about game nights, talks, retreats and outings to break people out of social isolation? Can't the parish sign people up to a seniors' walking club, getting them off their sofas and moving a few times a week? What about regular visits and phone calls to parishioners living on their own? If the parish wants a chance to prevent untreated depression in the pews, it's going to have to know its parishioners well enough to know who might be depressed.

Many parishes have helped people to form support groups for those trying to lose weight. Regular meetings of people who share the same struggles with weight and an unhealthy relationship with their refrigerator have been proven over and over to be far more effective than all the extreme diets screaming at us from magazine covers as we check out our groceries.

Renting the church basement out for weekly AA and Narcotics Anonymous meetings isn't a bad thing, but it isn't the same as directly helping parishioners who are struggling with alcohol and other addictions. It isn't the same as knowing parishioners well enough to refer them for counselling when needed.

If a lack of formal education is a risk factor for dementia, parish life probably won't make up for the schooling that aging parishioners should have had a generation or two previous. But parishes can offer people chances to learn new things – book clubs, art gallery tours, talks on church history and scripture. This isn't about replacing the school system or enrolling every Catholic for an M.Div. It is an opportunity to show people they can learn. Imagine you've always thought you can't. Your parish can show people they need not live their whole lives under the judgment of some long-dead elementary school teacher.

The extremely well-organized parish might find the resources to hire a parish nurse. An ambitious parish nurse might be able to bring in a diabetes educator once a week for consultations with parishioners. Even without a parish nurse, a parish in Ontario could type in "diabetes educator" at the Health Care Options website,[48] see what turns up and start phoning around to set up consultations. In the U.S., go to diabetescare.net to find state-by-state listings of diabetes educators.

One of the most profoundly Catholic things parishes can do to support the cognitive health of parishioners is to teach Christian meditation.[49] The World Community for Christian Meditation, based on the teaching of Benedictine monk Dom John Main, has chapters scattered across the globe. If there isn't one near you, they provide clear instructions about how to start one.[50] [51]

The research so far about whether regular meditation can effectively defend against dementia is ambiguous,[52] though it is certain it can't hurt. Ask a doctor what she does to maintain her cognitive health. Many meditate regularly.

Even if meditation doesn't prevent dementia, if a parish can lead its people to a serious, disciplined and profoundly spiritual practice, how could such a parish not be ready to care for people with dementia?

The dementia-ready parish is just a better parish.

# The Reality of Care

**Beyond the patient, who we're helping**

The most dementia-ready parish in the world, with the most detailed dementia plans and dedicated staff and volunteers, is not going to actually care for any dementia patients. The real caregivers will be daughters and sons, husbands, wives and extended family. In a few cases it will be lifelong neighbours and friends.

One in every four Canadians above the age of 15 cares for somebody with a significant disability.[53] There are more than 65 million American caregivers.[54] As our population ages and the tide of dementia rises, St. Elizabeth Health Care chief clinical officer Nancy Lefebre can see a time coming soon when it will be one in three Canadians caring for a family member.

In the U.S., caregivers of people with dementia put in an estimated 18.6 billion hours of unpaid labour in 2019, a contribution to the nation valued at nearly $244 billion. Two thirds of those caregivers are women.[55]

Your parish is no different from the rest of the country. Scan the pews and imagine every third or fourth person is praying with and for somebody who struggles against this disease. Imagine that for every third pew-sitter, there is someone waiting at home who absorbs their days in just ordinary daily care.

People with dementia might need help getting dressed. Cooking will one day be too complicated and dangerous for them. There comes a time when they can't drive anymore and even walking, they need to be accompanied whenever they leave the house. Keeping medications straight is difficult when you can't remember what you just did or what day of the week it is. From working the TV remote to opening and closing jam jars, managing tubes of toothpaste, the latches on windows and doors – all kinds of everyday objects and tasks become too difficult.

In the early stages, the help needed to get dementia patients through the day isn't complicated or technical or medical. But it is constant. If they need a shave, somebody has to shave them.[56] If they want to listen to music, somebody has to turn on the radio. If they want a nap, somebody has to guide them to a safe and comfortable place. If they want to talk to someone, they need someone there who can fill in the blanks of words they can't remember and who can gentle and calm them as their frustration rises.

At first, caregivers don't think they're doing anything special. They don't call themselves caregivers.

"They start helping out a parent or a spouse a little bit more than usual, and then they just kind of see that as something that family does for each other. They don't really think of themselves as a caregiver until they get quite far along in the journey," Lefebre told me. "It's often a quite significant change or crisis or tipping point that causes them to become totally overwhelmed with the demands of caregiving."

That's when they know they are caregivers. It is often a sign telling them they also need help. But where do they go?

Of course, the parish could pull together a list of phone numbers and websites for services available in their community. Parish volunteers of all kinds, from ushers to choir members, should know where to get a hold of that list. It should be on the parish website. It's a different list in every town, every province, every state.

Americans can go to the Alzheimer's Association website to speak with a caregiver specialist via live chat at alz.org/help-support/caregiving. They'll connect you with local and state agencies.

The Elizz suite of resources and services available from St. Elizabeth Healthcare[57] is a great starting point no matter where you are in Canada. They can help caregivers assess their situation and guide them to people and services that can help. Their website is full of practical advice and sensible, realistic encouragement.

"Right across Canada, you will hear people often talk about the complexities of navigating the health system," said Lefebre. The Elizz website and advisors available online or by phone can make it a little easier and a little clearer.

Politicians everywhere and of every political party have talked about increasing support and funding for home care. But none of these promises have made the system easier to navigate.

Approaching this system is also, frankly, frightening. Homecare services are not necessarily covered by provincial health insurance in Canada or private health insurance in the United States. How many daily personal support worker visits or weekly nursing visits would it take to bankrupt an average family?

These are the kinds of crises that can be better managed when dementia patients are diagnosed early and caregivers are plugged into supports well before they are overwhelmed.[58] The parish can't do those clinical assessments, but it can tell families who to talk to and where to go for help. Most of all, by talking openly and often about dementia, the parish can encourage caregivers to seek out assessments and talk to their parents or spouses about the cognitive decline they're seeing.[59]

At Providence Hospital in Toronto, Norm Dickenson told me about the support he gets from the Providence Adult Day Program[60] in caring for his wife, June. June has known for some time that she has Alzheimer's. She accepts that she needs special care. Twice a week, Norm drops June off at Providence for an afternoon of activities.

June has made friends at Providence – not just among the caregivers but also with other regulars in the program. The participants on her regular afternoons are organized into clubs. June is not a patient at Providence. She's a member of a club.

The Providence program is not on a hospital ward. It's in its own dedicated suite of rooms where participants are guided through crafts, get some exercise disguised as dance, are given spa treatments and have their hair styled. The men socialize over a glass of (dealcoholized) beer in the pub room. The telescope is popular. Music on iPods and photo albums remind them of experiences they had when they were young.

While June enjoys her afternoon out, Norm attends meetings with other husbands caring for their wives.

"That's the thing. We help each other," Norm told me.

Norm also uses his uninterrupted afternoons to do grocery shopping, house cleaning and other tasks. "Sometimes I just do nothing," he told me.

Parishes can't put on a medically supervised program in a safe, dedicated facility. If you suggest it, the diocesan liability lawyers and finance officers will break out in hives. And smaller communities in Canada or the U.S. don't have anything like Toronto's Providence Adult Day Program, or the kind of well-heeled corporate and family donors it took to build and staff the facility.

However, with not much more than volunteers, meeting rooms, email addresses and phone numbers, any parish can create a network of caregivers – groups like Norm's gang of husbands. If people can support each other, the parish should help them to do it.

But neither should the parish simply accept that their community can't have a Providence Adult Day Program. If the hospitals and nursing homes in your town don't have a facility where caregivers can bring their loved ones for an afternoon, or a day, or a night of respite, ask why. Pressure from a parish for better services can get action from local members of provincial Parliament, state senators, mayors, town councillors and hospital boards.

It might take years. It might be frustrating. But caregivers in your parish should never have to ask themselves who is on their side.

# Real Dying

## The new legal and cultural landscape

By the time this book is published, Canada will have a law that allows people in the early stages of dementia, or who fear a future diagnosis of dementia, to preordain that they should be killed when the disease gets really bad.

Washington State has had this legal option available for years.

Canada's definition of "really bad" will be whatever the patient says it is, whether it is losing their glasses three times in one day or the week they go mute and start choking on chocolate pudding. There will be no objective, medical standard that qualifies them for medical assistance in dying (MAiD). Doctors and healthcare institutions that refuse to ratify these patient choices may be tolerated by the new law, but professionally they are increasingly regarded as derelict in a supposed duty to comply with patient choices.

"This is a horrific thing that's happened to medicine," Sr. Nuala Kenny, emeritus professor of medicine and founder of the Dalhousie University department of bioethics, told me as Canada adopted its first Medical Assistance in Dying law. "This is a capitulation to a market model of medicine. It's the medicalization of suffering. It's the total rejection of the paschal mystery. But we don't live in a Christian world anymore."[61]

She's wrong about that. We do live in a Christian world, even when we fail to be Christian, even when we're not the majority and especially when we're not in control. Christ inaugurated the Christian world from the cross, bleeding and choking to death, gasping the words "Forgive them; for they do not know what they are doing" (Luke 23:34). Jesus was not in control – why should you be?

Christians will no longer have the law on their side as the prohibition against doctors helping their patients commit suicide falls in state after state. The questions before your parish and each of its families are these: How will they be Christian despite the law? And how will they be Christians with and for people who die of dementia? How will they be really present with and for parishioners with dementia before they die, then as they die and finally in memory of them after they die?

Legalized assisted dying has no effect on the basic facts of death. It's still our universal destiny. None of us are getting out of here alive. We are mere mortals.

Death is not more or less dignified depending on the state of your brain cells when your heart stops beating. Death by Alzheimer's or frontotemporal dementia or Parkinson's is just death. You are equally dead whether you die riddled with cancer, in a car crash or by lethal injection. Every death is death and only death.

Whether by suicide, on the battlefield or under a down comforter with a half-finished glass of sherry on the night table beside you, each death is unique. But the event is only unique because it relates to a unique life lived up to that point. There is no dying with dignity because dignity is a quality of life, not death.

Shanaaz Gokool, former executive director of Dying With Dignity Canada, used to insist in interviews with me that choosing when, where and how we die is a human right. Any infringement on this constitutionally protected right to choose is a violation of human dignity, Gokool told me. She fought hard to overcome Canada's first assisted dying law that said you had to be competent and asking for death at that moment when the doctor administers lethal drugs. To take away a patient's right to an assisted death because the disease killing them had already stolen their ability to give consent was, for Gokool, cruel injustice.

When Canada's new law passes, Gokool will get her way. Doctors will be able to assume the consent of patients with dementia. Given a legal instruction on paper, signed months or years before, doctors will be able to exercise their judgment in determining what the patient really wants. This judgment may run counter to the patient's inarticulate instinct, which causes her to recoil and cry out at the sight of the needle.

This will be our new definition of dignity. Patients will be strapped down, held down and overcome by younger and stronger doctors and nurses so that the medical professionals can inject lethal drugs into patients who sometime previous had feared one day becoming helpless. In their fear of an unknown future and a terrible disease, they cancelled it all, including themselves, with words on paper. The doctors, then, will respond not to the patient before them but to that piece of paper.

Dignity is not manufactured by exercising choice. If it was, we could shop our way to dignity, choosing the peach-scented body wash over the oatmeal-based sensitive skin formula. If choosing gave us dignity, then we in the 21st century who choose our careers, our homes, our spouses and our politics would all somehow be more dignified than 19th-century merchant sailors or 17th-century Russian serfs or, indeed, the landed gentry (*dvorianstvo*) who inherited the serfs and the land from their fathers and grandfathers. Neither serf nor lord had a choice. But their relative absence of choice made them neither more nor less human than we free and modern people swimming in a sea of choice. Their dignity quotient is no lower or higher because they lived when they did. Dignity scores did not rise if they ran away with the circus.

Dignity is not derived from choice. It is, rather, the precondition to meaningful choice. One must be fully human to make real human choices. Becoming human is not easy because it is not something anyone can do for or by themselves.[62] Before you can choose, you must be chosen and you must know yourself to be chosen.

You can choose to fall in love with a beautiful stranger on the subway. You can choose to be an Olympic shot putter or the prime minister of France. Such choices are exercises in fantasy or hubris or both – unless the stranger on the subway is in love with you, unless you have spent years competing and perfecting your shot put technique, unless you have spent your life leading your fellow French citizens to a better future, gaining their admiration and confidence.

It is not your choice that confers upon you the dignity of lover, athlete or leader. You have that dignity only if and when you are chosen. To be Christian is to know you are the fundamental choice of God, chosen to be part of the humanity embraced in Jesus' life, passion and resurrection. Choosing death – or, more precisely, choosing to be killed in a particular way at a particular time and in a particular setting – is like choosing to fall in love with the beautiful stranger on the subway. It is a choice absurdly exercised outside the context of being chosen. To compel others to put such a choice into effect is maniacal, tyrannical or, at best, narcissistic.

You have been chosen for life. This does not mean a choice for your unique, heroic path through life – the path effected by the power of your choices. It means your participation in all life. It means you have been chosen to be part of the life surrounding you, part of life as God created it.

Death does not choose you. If it did, then some would remain unchosen. But so far, everyone born has also died. Death is an event, not a person, and it doesn't choose. Choosing death isn't a genuine choice because it doesn't respond to any fundamental choice of God.[63]

To be chosen for life by God confers on every one of us the dignity of being human and sets the table for all of our human choices. This call and response of dignity between humans and God requires that if chosen for life we choose life, if chosen by God we choose God, if chosen to rejoice we rejoice with those who share our life, and if chosen to suffer we suffer with Christ.

Dignity is connection. Dignity is how we fit in. Dignity can only be measured in what we take from and give to other people. And we must be alive to do that.

Perhaps that sounds abstract or an exercise in philosophy. But for a parish full of people living with dementia, it is real and urgent. Parishioners with dementia have the same legal right as any other citizen to write out their death wish and file it with their lawyer and their doctor. I propose that parishes should do something about this.

The parish won't change this law and you can't take away someone's writing materials. But a dementia-ready parish can give people a sense that they are part of something. It can show people who don't have dementia or who find themselves in the early stages that they need not fear a future of cognitive decline. They need not fear it because they will still share in the life and love of a community.

The vocation of a Christian community is to live out God's fundamental choice – that choice to be incarnate and alive. It has to make that choice real in the lives of individuals and in the life of the community. The eucharist demands of the parish real presence. When Christ is present among us and with us, we know how to share life, overcome fear, rejoice together and weep with one another.

Cardinal Peter Turkson once told me, "We cannot live as a human society in our interconnectedness, in our interdependence, if we are not able to support and uphold one another ... The thing about assisted suicide or euthanasia or whatever you call it – how does it make for the due recognition of the dignity and the character of human life?"

Later that evening in 2016, Turkson delivered the annual John M. Kelly Lecture to faculty and students at the University of St. Michael's College. There he took a stab at answering his own question.

"No individual is an island," he said. "This is true in every aspect and phase of human life. Relationship is fundamental to being human. End-of-life provisions must not neglect this point."

Remember the bread and cup raised above the altar in memory of God made flesh. Precisely there, Christ is really present in that aspect and phase of human life. Because in his relationship with us he is risen. Our relationship with Christ, as individuals and as a parish, is also our relationship with those around us in the church and those in a nursing home three blocks away living with dementia.

Any society that would leave you stranded, isolated and alone to make your own faux dignity by shopping for the right timing, chemistry and setting for death – a society that would make death a consumer choice – has failed the dignity test. To confuse dignity with autonomy is to forget that meaningful autonomy depends on our relationship with other people. Freedom in a vacuum, freedom that cannot relate to other people, is not freedom. It's solitary confinement without the advantages of a jailer and a key.

The Second Vatican Council took dignity very seriously.

"Whatever is opposed to life itself, such as any type of murder, genocide, abortion, euthanasia or wilful self-destruction, whatever violates the integrity of the human person, such as mutilation, torments inflicted on body or mind, attempts to coerce the will itself; whatever insults human dignity, such as subhuman living conditions, arbitrary imprisonment, deportation, slavery, prostitution, the selling of women and children; as well as disgraceful working conditions, where men are treated as mere tools for profit, rather than as free and responsible persons; all these things and others of their like are infamies indeed. They poison human society, but they do more harm to those who practice them than those who suffer from the injury. Moreover, they are supreme dishonour to the Creator," said *Gaudium et Spes* (27), the Pastoral Constitution of the Church in the Modern World.

We cannot choose our way into dignity or out of it. We can honour the choice God has already made.

At L'Arche, people have learned to embrace their dignity and humanity by sharing their lives. Sr. Sue Mosteller, the great writer and collaborator with Henri Nouwen who lived a big chunk of her life at L'Arche, told me about the day a Muslim core member of the Daybreak community north of Toronto died. The Muslim tradition is to bury people the day they die. That was a problem for this community. L'Arche tradition and Muslim tradition were at odds.

"We always gather around the body and we spend time and we tell stories. We had no time. She died on the feast of Eid. She had to be buried that day," Mosteller told me. "They (mosque officials) just said to us, 'Everybody come to the mosque.' Of course they (Muslims) don't open the casket. They don't do anything like that. They took us upstairs for the feast of Eid and they were celebrating in the mosque. Afterwards, everybody in the mosque was invited to come to the gym because this person had died, and they were going to have the funeral."

The community at the mosque was deeply grateful for the years their daughter had spent with L'Arche. They wanted to meet her friends and welcome them at their mosque as she had been welcomed by L'Arche. It was the only dignified thing to do.

"The casket was there. So we all sat down (in the gym)," recalled Mosteller. "The Imam came and said, 'These are the people of Daybreak. They always take time and we're going to do something we don't usually do. We're going to open the casket and give them some time to tell their stories and to gather around her body so they can really live this as they usually live it.'"

A quarter century on, as Mosteller told me this story, she was still amazed.

"Can you believe that?" she said. "It was just for half an hour. And 40 of us (were) there, going up and telling these stories and laughing so hard about something that happened during her time. And then we were crying because she was gone. Somebody just burst out crying, saying I can't stand that she has died."

It's hard to be solemn at L'Arche, but after the stories and tributes around the casket, the gym in the mosque complex turned solemn.

"Two hundred people sitting in the mosque, just silent with us," said Mosteller. "And at the end they just said to the other people, if anybody would like to come up and view the body. So some of the people from the mosque came up. Then they closed the casket. Then they carried her out to bury her. But… That's not just talking. That's kindness and that's relationships and generosity."

The L'Arche community brought its dignity to that funeral. The Muslim community responded with its dignity. Dignity is connection. Dignity is a life shared and a life recognized.

The dementia-ready parish will not let people die alone. The dementia-ready parish will lift up every connection the dead had to their parish in their lifetimes. The dementia-ready parish will not allow their passing to go by unspoken, uncelebrated. But all of this must begin long before they die.

Despite the sorrow and loss people with dementia experience as memories fade, the more life is shared, the more dignity they and we carry into death.

# Really Caring

## Courage in our encounter with dementia

Your parish cares. There is no caring deficit. But we have atomized care, so that care and the carers are suspended in isolation, hovering in the atmosphere near and far from your parish.

For the parish to recapture care, to draw this dispersed community of care into itself, it must attract the carers. To attract caregivers, care for them. Be there for them. Be a real presence upon which they may rely.

"If you are a community that really supports those folks out there, they're going to support you," Michelle O'Rourke told me. "It's a two-way street. If they feel that their parish cares about them, they're going to continue to stay connected. They're going to continue to give. They're going to be a part of this vibrant parish."

O'Rourke is the author of *Healthy Caregiving: Perspectives for Caring Professionals in Company with Henri Nouwen.*[64] She also spent years working for the diocese of London, Ontario, helping parishes organize and prepare volunteers to carry on the mission of the church among the isolated and vulnerable, beyond the walls of the church.

"Parishes have to see their mission as something that is outward, instead of just maintenance," she said.

She doesn't pretend this is easy.

"It takes gumption. It takes passion. It takes a desire to put things in place so that you have some visitors in place – whether they're doing it over the phone or they're doing it with personal visits – to really support your folks who are stuck at home."

The first step is to find out who the caregivers are in the parish.

"They are in an unchosen profession," explained O'Rourke. "They are kind of thrown into it."

There are concrete, genuine dangers to not supporting these people.

"Compassion fatigue is what happens to people who don't get supported, who get burned out when they're caregiving," she said.

Few parishes would question the value of forming and supporting a bereavement group, a refugee committee or a seniors' social circle. There should be no question that caregivers also deserve space, time and parish resources.

"Trying to arm people with as much support and resources as we can is huge," said O'Rourke.

It's not huge because it's good marketing for the parish. Caregivers are not a key demographic. No parish should do this so that the parish might become an essential provider of valued services. The church is the body of Christ, not a social enterprise. Rather, it is through caregivers that the church of Christ extends its real presence out to those who are living the paschal mystery in the hidden places of our world.

Penetrating these hidden places inches us toward what Pope Francis has called a culture of encounter. It causes us to face up to our neighbours and to ourselves.

"To speak of a 'culture of encounter' means that we, as a people, should be passionate about meeting others, seeking points of contact, building bridges, planning a project that includes everyone," Pope Francis writes in the encyclical *Fratelli Tutti* (216). "This becomes an aspiration and a style of life. The subject of this culture is the people, not simply one part of society that would pacify the rest with the help of professional and media resources."

Pope Francis' culture of encounter presupposes the real presence. But the pope is under no illusion that the real presence can be taken for granted. It must be cherished, built and maintained with daily prayer, discernment and toil.

"Consumerist individualism has led to great injustice. Other persons come to be viewed simply as obstacles to our own serene existence; we end up treating them as annoyances and we become increasingly aggressive. This is even more the case in times of crisis, catastrophe and hardship, when we are tempted to think in terms of the old saying, 'every man for himself.' Yet even then, we can choose to cultivate kindness. Those who do so become stars shining in the midst of darkness" (*Fratelli Tutti*, 222).

Your parish can be that star in the midst of darkness by encountering dementia with and through the caregivers.

"The real presence is sitting yourself down beside that person and listening," said O'Rourke. "It's about being present before you try to fix something. We're not there to try to fix things. We can't fix dementia. We can't fix the fact that caregivers are going to get burned out. But we can support them. We can try to arm them with things so that they don't get burned out as quickly and so that they know they don't have to do this alone."

This isn't a strategy. It's a spirituality, Sr. Lucy Bethel of the Providence Spirituality Centre in Kingston, Ontario, told me. Bethel lives with sisters experiencing dementia and she encounters dementia in her work as a spiritual director.

"I often find myself on the journey, accompanying persons with dementia," she wrote in an email.

Bethel never wonders whether retreats and spiritual direction are valuable for people wrestling with memory loss.

"As I work with women and men who are experiencing a decline in mental capacity and loss of memories, I find consolation, you might say, in the light of their spirits as they share their hearts and souls with me in our one-on-one sessions together," she said. "I witness the light of God within each one of them – a light that never diminishes."

Our encounter with dementia is first of all an encounter with human beings. It is not primarily about the disease. It is about our own loneliness and isolation coming into contact with the loneliness and isolation of others.

"Whether we are rich or poor, famous or unknown, fully abled or disabled, we all share the fear of being left alone and abandoned, a fear that remains hidden under the surface of our self-composure," Henri Nouwen wrote in *Our Greatest Gift: A Meditation on Dying and Caring*.[65] "It is rooted much more deeply than in the possibility of not being liked or loved by people. Its deepest root lies in the possibility of not being loved at all, of not belonging to anything that lasts, or being swallowed up by a dark nothingness – yes, of being abandoned by God."

God does not abandon us, even if our memories slip away. And if God will not abandon his creatures, we may not abandon one another.

"Caring, therefore, is being present to people as they fight this ultimate battle, a battle that becomes evermore real and intense," Nouwen writes.

This isn't a burden we can bear alone.

"We shouldn't try to care by ourselves," Nouwen said. "Care is not an entrance test. We should, whenever possible, care together with others."

We have these parishes and we have this church so that we can be a community of care bound to one another in the real presence of the body of Christ. To have hope is to encounter Christ's presence in mystery, in concrete action and in our midst. Respond to that presence, Christ's presence, with and for people with dementia.

# Sources

## Confronting Reality

1. Public Health Agency of Canada: https://www.canada.ca/en/public-health/services/publications/diseases-conditions/dementia-highlights-canadian-chronic-disease-surveillance.html
2. Royal Society of Canada, Restoring Trust: COVID-19 and The Future of Long-Term Care (June 2020). https://rsc-src.ca/en/research-and-reports/covid-19-policy-briefing/long-term-care/restoring-trust-covid-19-and-future
3. https://www.alzheimers.net/resources/alzheimers-statistics
4. https://www.alz.org/news/2020/primary-care-physicians-on-the-front-lines-of-diag
5. https://www.alz.org/news/2020/primary-care-physicians-on-the-front-lines-of-diag
6. https://www.weforum.org/agenda/2016/02 this-is-how-much-dementia-will-cost-the-world
7. https://alzheimer.ca/en/Home/About-dementia/What-is-dementia/Dementia-numbers
8. https://rsc-src.ca/en/restoring-trust-covid-19-and-future-long-term-care
9. https://en.novalis.ca/products/prayers-for-dementia-ct2020?_pos=75&_sid=99b03a3fc&_ss=r
10. https://alzheimer.ca/en/hpe/dfc
11. https://www.alz.org
12. https://www.alz.org/greatermissouri/volunteer/faith_outreach#:~:text=Faith%20Outreach%20Ambassadors%20are%20trained,Association%20for%20services%20and%20support

## Jesus Knows Our Reality

13. https://www.youtube.com/watch?v=OVhA01J0Zsg

## The Reality Code

14. https://www.youtube.com/watch?v=VuDtkt3lKsU&list=PLSq1p8iDbDSrejNkHbk9iOLKeoqb0xTDR
15. Pope John Paul II (1993), *Veritatis Splendor*, 108.
16. Pope Francis (2015), *Laudato Si'*, 22.
17. https://www.youtube.com/watch?v=BpzVFdDeWyo
18. https://www.scientificamerican.com/article/five-types-of-research-underexplored-until-recently-could-produce-alzheimers-treatments
19. https://www.brightfocus.org/alzheimers-disease/infographic/amyloid-plaques-and-neurofibrillary-tangles
20. https://alzheimer.ca/en/Home/About-dementia/Alzheimers-disease
21. https://www.webmd.com/alzheimers/guide/making-diagnosis-tests#1
22. https://www.beingpatient.com/new-alzheimers-eye-exam-research

23 https://www.nytimes.com/2020/07/28/health/alzheimers-blood-test.html?campaign_id=60&emc=edit_na_20200728&instance_id=0&nl=breaking-news&ref=headline&regi_id=53320403&segment_id=34565&user_id=eca1d4bc9bc8feba33093e6ac1a3b632
24 https://www.ajc.com/news/national/how-does-alzheimer-disease-kill-you/G86og0asuVjgPhv5nSto8N/#:~:text=The%20vast%20majority%20of%20those,lungs%20that%20develops%20into%20pneumonia
25 https://alzheimer.ca/en/bc/Living-with-dementia/Caring-for-someone/Understanding-symptoms/Changes-in-mood
26 https://alzheimer.ca/en/bc/Living-with-dementia/Caring-for-someone/Understanding-symptoms
27 https://alzheimer.ca/en/bc/Living-with-dementia/Day-to-day-living/Safety/Wandering-and-dementia
28 https://alzheimer.ca/en/Home/About-dementia/Dementias/Vascular-Dementia
29 https://www.drugs.com/drug-class/cholinesterase-inhibitors.html
30 https://alzheimer.ca/en/Home/About-dementia/Dementias/Mild-Cognitive-Impairment
31 https://www.mayoclinic.org/diseases-conditions/alzheimers-disease/expert-answers/vitamin-d-alzheimers/faq-20111272#:~:text=Research%20suggests%20that%20people%20with,and%20other%20forms%20of%20dementia
32 https://alzheimer.ca/en/Home/About-dementia/What-is-dementia/Shattering-the-myths
33 https://alzheimer.ca/en/bc/About-dementia/Dementias/Rarer-forms-of-dementia

## The Caring Reality

34 http://islandcatholicnews.ca/news/2016/10/nursing-pioneer-sister-simone-roach-created-theory-caring
35 https://www.theglobeandmail.com/news/national/nursing-pioneer-sister-simone-roach-created-theory-of-caring/article30930516
36 The Baltimore Catechism couldn't get much beyond a capacity to "discover our sins and learn to fear the punishment they deserve."

## Reality Out There

37 https://www.cihi.ca/en/dementia-in-canada/dementia-across-the-health-system/dementia-in-long-term-care#:~:text=Within%20long%2Dterm%20care%20homes,or%20trauma)%20was%2087%25
38 https://alz-journals.onlinelibrary.wiley.com/doi/full/10.1002/alz.12068
39 Catechism of the Catholic Church, 1362–1390.
40 https://www.nytimes.com/2018/01/17/world/europe/uk-britain-loneliness.html

## Real Liturgy

41 Eucharistic Prayer II.
42 Gilles Mongeau, *Embracing Wisdom: The Summa Theologiae and Spiritual Pedagogy* (Pontifical Institute of Medieval Studies, 2015).

43  For more on the practice of memory in prayer, see Michael Swan, *Written on My Heart: Classic Prayers in the Modern World* (Novalis, 2020).

## Physical Reality

44  https://www.nia.nih.gov/health/alzheimers-disease-genetics-fact-sheet#:~:text=APOE%20%CE%B54%20increases%20risk%20for,3%20percent%20carry%20two%20copies

45  https://alzheimer.ca/en/Home/About-dementia/Alzheimer-s-disease/Risk-factors#RiskFactorsYouCannotChange

46  https://www.canada.ca/en/public-health/services/publications/diseases-conditions/diabetes-canada-highlights-chronic-disease-surveillance-system.html

47  https://www.cdc.gov/diabetes/library/features/diabetes-stat-report.html

48  https://www.ontario.ca/locations/health

49  https://www.wccm.org/content/meditatio-meditation-and-science

50  https://www.wccm.org/content/wccm-meditation-groups

51  Laurence Freeman, *Christian Meditation: Your Daily Practice* (Novalis, 2007).

52  https://www.youtube.com/watch?v=RpzTYpXpSU0

## The Reality of Care

53  https://www150.statcan.gc.ca/n1/pub/75-006-x/2020001/article/00001-eng.htm

54  https://www.apa.org/pi/about/publications/caregivers/faq/statistics#:~:text=According%20to%20estimates%20from%20the,an%20ill%20or%20disabled%20relative

55  https://alz-journals.onlinelibrary.wiley.com/doi/full/10.1002/alz.12068

56  https://www.youtube.com/watch?v=OJ12gWOtw50

57  https://elizz.com

58  https://www.youtube.com/watch?v=0fcGjltroek and https://www.youtube.com/watch?v=FJQXbgm8JyA

59  https://elizz.com/caregiver-resources/how-to-talk-to-your-parent-about-dementia-symptoms

60  https://www.providence.on.ca/programs-services/adult-day-program

## Real Dying

61  Dr. Kenny's passionate, Christian response to the state's abandonment of the dying is laid out in Nuala Kenny, *Recovering the Art of Dying: How Jesus' Experience and Our Stories Reveal a New Vision of Compassionate Care* (Novalis, 2018).

62  Jean Vanier, *Becoming Human* (House of Anansi Press, 2008). The whole damn book.

63  As a matter of fact, God asked us not to eat of that tree in the middle of the garden.

## Really Caring

64  Michelle O'Rourke, *Healthy Caregiving: Perspectives for Caring Professionals in Company with Henri Nouwen* (Novalis, 2020).

65  Henri Nouwen, *Our Greatest Gift: A Meditation on Dying and Caring* (HarperOne, 2009).